MICHAEL

CW00434627

LIES! LIES! LIES!

EXPOSING MYTHS ABOUT THE **REAL JESUS**

INTER-VARSITY PRESS
Norton Street, Nottingham NG7 3HR, England
Email: ivp@ivpbooks.com
Website: www.ivpbooks.com

First published 2009

British Library Cataloguing in Publication Data
A catalogue record for this book is available from the British Library.

ISBN 978–1–84474–391–9

Typeset by CRB Associates, Potterhanworth, Lincolnshire
Printed and bound in Great Britain by Ashford Colour Press Ltd, Gosport,
Hampshire

*Inter-Varsity Press publishes Christian books that are true to the Bible and that
communicate the gospel, develop discipleship and strengthen the church for its mission
in the world.*

*Inter-Varsity Press is closely linked with the Universities and Colleges Christian
Fellowship, a student movement connecting Christian Unions in universities and
colleges throughout Great Britain, and a member movement of the International
Fellowship of Evangelical Students. Website: www.uccf.org.uk*

Michael Green has done a superb demolition job. He does not just rebut the untruthful travesties about Jesus, he blows them sky high.
Jonathan Aitken, author, broadcaster and former Cabinet Minister

Michael Green does a scholarly job addressing modern day 'prophets' (i.e. Dan Brown, *The Da Vinci Code*, Christopher Hitchens, *God is Not Great*), as well as boldly giving response to Muslim's attack on the Scriptures and Christ's crucifixion. This book is a must-read for Christian University students defending their faith and a challenge to sceptics who doubt the validity of the greatest story ever told.
Michael Mehaffie, Campus Director, Campus Crusade for Christ at N.C. State, North Carolina

Michael Green is in sparkling form. His book crackles with energy as he deals with many of the popular half-truths and untruths about Jesus. A book to encourage, inspire and motivate. Above all, a book to believe.

It's all too easy for Christians to half-believe what our culture wants us to believe about our faith, namely, that it lacks intelligent credibility. It's time for Christians to re-state our case. There is nowhere better to start than with Jesus, and no-one better qualified to state the case than Michael Green. Truth matters, and this book shows why it matters and how it can be restated persuasively and with verve.
The Right Reverend John Pritchard, Bishop of Oxford

Canon Dr Michael Green is one of the world's leading evangelists. The author of more than 40 books, I have seldom met anyone with so much energy. As a former principal of St John's College, Nottingham, and Rector of St Aldate's, Oxford, he is a respected theologian, yet his books are accessible to all. [After nearly four decades,] he continues to travel worldwide on speaking and preaching engagements. He is an inspiration to us all.
Rev. Nicky Gumbel, vicar of Holy Trinity Brompton and pioneer of the Alpha Course

A powerful and exciting book by one of Britain's leading Christian scholars that shows the shallowness of contemporary thinking concerning Jesus Christ.

Lord Carey, 103rd Archbishop of Canterbury

CONTENTS

INTRODUCTION

There is a remarkable and regrettable characteristic in human nature. When we see something noble or beautiful, for a while we admire it, and then we try to pull it down. It is thus with sports stars. So long as they perform well we idolize them. As soon as they show signs of frailty we rubbish them.

The highest standard of life that has ever been shown is that of Jesus Christ. He has won multi-millions to his allegiance. But he has also stirred up the fierce opposition of those who want to drag him in the mire or pull him down to their level. All manner of accusations are made against him, and you meet a sample of them in this book.

Often the best tactic for Christians is to ignore the slights and lies that are levelled against Jesus in films, books, articles and TV programmes. These generally have a short life, and Christians have better things to do than to be endlessly defending Jesus against a raft of calumnies. But every now and again it is time to break silence. It is time to show how ill-placed those lies and accusations are, and to revel afresh in the sheer attractiveness of the person of Jesus.

Lord Hailsham, former Lord Chancellor of the British parliament, put it well in *The Door Wherein I Went*: 'The first thing we must learn about him is that we should have been absolutely entranced by his company. Jesus was irresistibly attractive. What they crucified was a young man, vital, full of life and the joy of it, the Lord of life itself, and even more the Lord of laughter, someone so utterly attractive that people followed him for the sheer fun of it. We need to recapture the vision of this glorious and happy man whose mere presence filled his companions with delight. No pale Galilean he, but a veritable Pied Piper of Hamelin who would have the children laughing all around him and squealing with pleasure and joy as he picked them up.'

John Lennon denied that Jesus was God, but was attracted to him – he saw him as 'probably a very hip guy'. He was fascinated by Franco Zeffirelli's portrayal in the film, *Jesus of Nazareth*.

I believe that the recapturing of the truth about Jesus, and the return of society towards the ideals he taught and embodied, is the greatest, perhaps the only hope, for our civilization. For nearly two thousand years the ideals of civility, respect for life, love, truth, honesty, gentleness and purity have been drawn to a large extent from the life and teaching of Jesus of Nazareth. The Christian tradition, coupled, since the fall of Constantinople in AD 1453, with the humanism derived from Greece and Rome, has been the standard for public and private life. Often denied, often abused, it has remained the ideal. But now it is being assailed on every side.

In our postmodern age both truth and morality are at a discount. Violence is everywhere on the increase. There is little respect for person or property. The politicians debate whether more police on the streets or longer sentences will solve it. But of course these expedients are nothing more than band-aid on the wound that has gone so deep into the soul of post-Christian Europe. A 'New Atheism' has arisen, even more virulent than the old. Professors like Richard Dawkins and Peter Atkins in Oxford, journalists like Christopher Hitchens, are passionate in their hatred of anything religious, and especially Christianity.

But the opposition to religion as a civilizing influence has cut more deeply still. John Gray, formerly Professor of European Thought at the London School of Economics, has written a challenge to his fellow atheists in his book *Straw*

Dogs – Thoughts on Humans and Other Animals. He agrees with them that Christianity is rubbish and the God of the Bible mere superstition, but he chides them for not going far enough. Humanism, the dominant ideology in the West is, he maintains, simply Christianity in a secular form which has replaced the idea of God's providence with that of human progress.

Gray writes, 'Christians understood history as a story of sin and redemption. Humanism is the transformation of this Christian doctrine of salvation into a project of universal emancipation. The idea of progress is the secular version of the Christian belief in providence . . . It rests on the belief that the growth of knowledge and the advance of the species go together – if not now, then in the long run.'

But he emphatically resists this illusion. 'Knowledge does not make us free. It leaves us as we have always been, prey to every kind of folly.' He is a rigid Darwinian. Human beings are mere animals – 'only currents in the drift of genes'. The problem with humanism, as he sees it, is not due to its atheistic and Darwinian roots, but that it has not been true to those roots.

A truly naturalistic view of the world for Gray leaves no room for secular hope. 'Darwin showed that humans are like other animals; humanists claim they are not. Humanists insist that by using our knowledge we can control our environment and flourish as never before.' He continues, 'But if Darwin's theory of natural selection is true, this is impossible. The human mind serves evolutionary success, not truth. To think otherwise is to resurrect the pre-Darwinian error that humans are different from all other animals.' The trouble with his fellow atheists is, he maintains, that they have not given up 'Christianity's cardinal error – the belief that humans are radically different from all other animals'.

From this depressing premise Gray fearlessly draws a number of conclusions. First, that human history has no meaning or significance. Second, that persons do not matter – they are only animals, after all. Third, that we are not responsible for what we do – 'the upshot of neuroscientific research is that we cannot be the authors of our acts'. And finally we must abandon the notion of morality, which he sees as an ugly superstition.

And all this, if you please, from one who was Professor of European Thought!

Humanism will not save our civilization, based as it is on the assumption that human beings are not special, but are merely animals. Does it not depress you to think that this is how one of the most highly educated human beings in the country evaluates fellow humans – as mere animals, with no morals to restrain them and no hope to sustain? What future has a civilization governed by such assumptions?

Atheism will not save our civilization. Following the philosophy of Nietzsche that might is right, atheist dictators like Hitler, Lenin, Stalin, Pol Pot, Mao and Mugabe have liquidated multi-millions of victims in order to impose their will. How current atheists can claim that their creed brings emancipation when it can just as easily lead to mass murder, as it has in the past century on a magisterial scale, simply astonishes me. We shall gain no help from that quarter.

Jean-Paul Sartre described our society as being 'on a shattered and deserted stage, without a script, director, prompter or audience' – where everyone improvises their own part. Pretty near the mark, is it not? The humorous film maker Woody Allen observed, 'More than at any time in history, mankind face a crossroads: one path leads to despair and utter hopelessness, the other to extinction. Let us pray that we may have the wit to choose correctly!'

One of the great prophets of our century has been Alexander Solzhenitsyn. This was his evaluation of what had happened in his homeland, Russia, during his lifetime. 'If I were asked to formulate as concisely as I could the main cause of the ruinous Revolution which has swallowed up some sixty million of our people, I could not put it more accurately than this: *men have forgotten God*. That is why all this has happened. And Godlessness is the first step to the gulag.' Solzhenitsyn had himself spent years in the gulag, and he knew what he was talking about.

There is one direction in which our civilization might look, if it cherishes hopes of a future. The ideal for human life is not beyond us. The ideal has lived. It is, of course, Jesus. He has had greater influence for good than any other person who has ever inhabited this planet. He has transformed the lives and characters of countless millions. It was so in the early church, with the radical change of people like Saul of Tarsus (Paul) and Simon Peter, James the brother of Jesus and Philip the evangelist. It remains so still.

Only today I was reading of the massive life-change in a man called Shane Taylor. For many years he was considered one of the most dangerous prisoners in Britain's jails. Originally imprisoned for attempted murder, he had his sentence extended for four years when he attacked a prison officer with a broken glass. The incident provoked a riot. He tells of how he was regarded as such a subversive and dangerous influence in the prison that his cell door could not be opened at times unless there were six or seven prison officers in full riot gear present. Taylor stumbled by mistake into an Alpha course, which was being held in the prison. This remarkable introductory course to Christianity in due course led him to trust Jesus Christ, as it has led thousands more.

Hardened criminal though he was, Taylor came to see what Jesus Christ had done for him on the cross, and in due course made his response. He wrote of this experience: 'I felt like I was in this room where although there was natural light, somebody switched on another light and everything became suddenly clearer than before. It felt as if I'd had an invisible layer covering my eyes and it was rubbed away. In that split second I knew it was real. I knew God existed. I knew Jesus had touched me and that I was going to live for him for ever.' Needless to say his fellow inmates, his warders and even his mother (when he was released from prison a year later) were very cynical about this supposed change in his life. But the proof of the pudding is in the eating. All of them were ultimately convinced.

This man who had spent most of his adult life in prison, returning time after time upon reoffending, has gone straight, is happily married, is in full employment, and is deeply involved in the life of his local church. His drug dealing, violence, stealing, and swearing are gone. He has made peace with someone he stabbed. He has learnt to forgive. Gradually Christian character has taken root and is growing in him.

I should love him to meet Professor John Gray, whom I quoted earlier. I do not think he would be very impressed by Gray's position that 'the upshot of neuroscientific research is that we cannot be the authors of our acts' or that 'persons do not matter – they are only animals'. Taylor is well aware of his responsibility and guilt for the actions he perpetrated. In days gone by he may have thought of men and women as mere animals who did not matter. Now he sees them as made in the image of God and for that reason worthy of respect. Which viewpoint offers more hope for the future of humanity in general and individuals in particular?

Now of course not everyone's encounter with Christ is like that of Shane Taylor. Though Christ is the way to God there are many paths to Christ. Taylor is just one example of the transforming power of Jesus Christ. And does not society desperately need to get in touch afresh with that divine, life-changing power? Can you see atheism changing a person for the better like that? Can you see prison doing it? On the contrary, most come out of prison worse and more criminal than when they went in – and the statistics prove it. But the glory of the gospel is that Jesus Christ has been making that sort of change to individuals and societies for centuries.

But let us be clear about one thing. It is the full-blooded Jesus of the New Testament, both human and divine, crucified and risen, who brings about this transformation. And he has become subject to enormous scorn and insult in the sceptical, materialistic West. Can you imagine what the Muslim world would have done had Muhammad been attacked and publicly slandered as Jesus has repeatedly been in recent decades? But I am convinced that the calumnies put out against him are lies. They are put forward by people who hate what he stands for and are determined to rubbish him if they can. But they will not withstand critical examination. Of course, not all doubts about Jesus are motivated by arrogance and hatred, and honest doubters will, I hope, find this book illuminating and reassuring.

This book is written in the conviction that the person and teaching of Jesus offers the most realistic hope for human destiny, both personal and collective. That is why, in what follows, I have tried to peel away layers of untruth and misunderstanding that keep many from considering his claims and recognizing his worth. Read on and make up your own mind, for the issues are momentous.

1. THE JESUS WE THOUGHT WE KNEW

If you say a word against Muhammad, the whole Muslim world can erupt. Witness the global fury over the Danish cartoons of Muhammad with a rocket in his head-dress. But a woman working in the airline industry wears a cross to work and is forced to remove it or lose her job. Another, a nurse, is suspended from her job for asking a patient if she would like a prayer to help her healing. And this is in Europe. There is something profoundly unequal going on here!

During recent years there have been countless smears against Jesus of Nazareth, the founder of the Christian faith. He is portrayed as the witty rabbi, the travelling salesman, the paramour of Mary Magdalene, the homosexual, the clown, the wandering charismatic prophet, and the impostor who never rose from the grave. Christians generally do not reply to allegations like this. They put up with the name of Jesus being dragged in the mud and used as a common swear word. But these repeated attacks can gradually erode the confidence of believers, and make it more difficult for others to join the Christian community because of the nagging fear that the foundations of the faith cannot withstand serious examination. So I propose in this short book to examine some of the current assaults on the person of Jesus and assess their credibility.

Before doing so, however, I must in this opening chapter outline the picture of Jesus which has been current in the churches all over the world from earliest days. That will give us an initial starting point for measuring the various arguments by which he is dismissed or marginalized. Many who attack the source of Christian belief put up a straw man, which simply will not do.

We possess four substantive accounts of the life and death of this remarkable person. All were written within a few decades of his death – something extremely unusual in the ancient world. Even more remarkable is the brand new type of literature they represent. It is known as 'gospel', meaning 'good news'. Not biography, though it contains biographical material. Not history, though it is rooted in history. But something entirely novel: gospel. The word, a rare one in the Greek language which was the *lingua franca* of the ancient world by the first century AD, resonated with both Jewish and secular readers. The Jew would think of the good news of Messianic salvation, or national rescue, predicted by the prophets, for which the nation had long been waiting. The secular reader would think of the way the word was used of the good news of the Emperor's birthday or perhaps of a special occasion when the Emperor might come to visit his city. The four evangelists, or Gospel writers, took this word over and applied it to someone whom they saw as greater than the Emperor. He had indeed come to visit a part of his world, and had delivered that rescue for which the Jews had been waiting, albeit not in the manner they were expecting.

From the earliest days, and certainly before the end of the first century, the four Gospels of Matthew, Mark, Luke and John were established as the core documents of this new faith, enshrining the good news about who Jesus was and what he accomplished.

Who was Jesus?

Who was he, then? The Gospel writers let us know their convictions from the very start. Matthew and Luke tell us that he was truly human, born of a young Jewish girl called Mary, and yet that he shared God's nature as well. They claim that Mary's womb was made alive by the Spirit of the one and only God, the Creator of the universe. Mark's Gospel starts abruptly, 'The beginning of the gospel about Jesus Christ, the Son of God.' And John's Gospel uses philosophical language with much resonance both in Greek and Jewish circles, in opening with: 'In the beginning was the Word, and the Word was with God, and the Word *was* God . . . ' The writer continues with awe and wonder: 'The Word became flesh and made his dwelling among us. We have seen his glory, the glory of the One and Only, who came from the Father' (1:14). He concludes his introduction to the Gospel thus, straining the boundaries of language: 'No one has ever seen God, but God the One and Only, who is at the Father's side, has made him known' (1:18).

So, each in their own way, the four Gospel writers make plain, from the outset of their account, their settled conviction that Jesus was not only human but shared the nature of God himself. As much of the divine as could be embodied in a human being dwelt in him. That was their claim – nothing less. It took them a long time and a massive struggle to reach that belief. After all, they were Jews, and the Jews were as passionate (and militant) monotheists as any Muslim is today. For the Jew, as for the Muslim, it was and remains total blasphemy to put anyone or anything on the same level as God.

Over a period of some two thousand years, the Jewish nation had rejected the widespread view that every tribe had its own god: they had become united in the belief that there was just one God, the God of the whole earth. The Romans, who took over the country in AD 6, had to learn to respect what to them seemed a ridiculously narrow-minded religion. Time and again there were riots and fatalities if the Romans brought any suspicion of idolatry, like legionary standards embossed with the image of the Emperor, into Jerusalem. So it was highly improbable that these first disciples of Jesus the carpenter should regard him as anything more than a fine man.

In due course, as we shall see, they simply could not confine him to the category of 'mere human'. All the more so in the light of his claims. This humble carpenter teacher actually claimed at least three things which properly belonged to God alone. He claimed to forgive sins. He claimed the right to accept worship. And he claimed that at the last day he would be the Judge of humankind. Totally crazy claims – unless they were true. And when those claims were backed up, as they were, by a matchless life and the miracles he performed, they began to be driven to the conclusion, so contrary to their assumptions and so shattering to their intellect, that God had indeed invaded our world in the person of Jesus in order to do something very special for his people.

The purpose of Jesus' life

He came to teach
If the first followers of Jesus believed him to be divine, then what did they think he had come to do? It is plain from all the Gospels that the authority of Jesus' teaching enthralled them. It was so exciting that people willingly dropped out of work to go and listen to him. Moreover, it brought to a climax the teaching they had inherited through the Jewish Law and the prophets.

He loved to speak about the kingdom of God – what life would be like if God was really enthroned as king in human lives. He spoke about God not as an absent dictator but as a loving father, ready to welcome his prodigal children back home. He spoke of the supreme quality of love, even for enemies. He called men and women to come and follow him.

Much of his public teaching adopted a style previously almost unknown – parables, or stories with a deeper meaning, which grabbed the attention of the hearers and forced them to reflect on what it might mean for them. It was immensely attractive. It made God very real. But it was also authoritative.

The reaction we find in Mark's Gospel after Jesus' first teaching was this: 'The people were amazed at his teaching, because he taught them as one who had authority, not as the teachers of the law' (Mark 1:22). The teachers of the law, the scribes, were the clergy of the day. And, like modern scholars, they constantly appealed to others as authorities. But Jesus never did this. Instead he coined a phrase which carries its own authority: 'Truly, truly I tell you.' Here was a man who did not speculate about the things of God. He knew. And people recognized it.

He came to embody God's kingly rule

But it was not just the authority of his teaching which had such an impact on Jesus' first followers. It was the authority of his deeds. Who was this young layman who could walk into the temple and challenge the high priest's domain by breaking up the crooked market that had developed there and by sending the traders packing? Who was this who could say to a paralyzed man 'Stretch out your hand' and immediately restore it to health? Who was this who could drive out the dark forces that were ruining a man's life and making him gash himself with stones as he eked out a shadowy, tormented existence among tombs? Who was this who could address a storm as if it were a living thing, and bid it cease its raging? Who was this who could bid his followers with cool confidence to go feed five thousand hungry people with five little buns and a few local fish? Who was this who could face the Roman governor, the man who claimed the power of life and death over Jesus, and calmly say that he could have no power over him whatsoever unless it was allowed him by God? All these acts are documented in the vivid pages of the Gospels. Read them and see!

What a man! In the light of such positive and authoritative action, no wonder his followers began to regard him as more than man.

We shall need to reflect more fully on the topic later, but a word must be said here about the miracles of Jesus. They figure prominently in the story told by these four writers of the Gospels. We find Jesus healing sick people, all sorts of them – the blind, the deaf, the paralyzed, even the supreme outcasts of the day, the lepers. It was a demonstration not just of divine compassion but the fact that God's long-promised kingdom had broken in. These miracles were not conjuring tricks or attempts to show off. They were occasioned by human need and were visible signs of who Jesus was and what life in the kingdom of God might look like.

The same point about Jesus' divine rule was made by the many accounts we have of his dealing with demonic forces. The Bible is clear that there is a devil, a supreme anti-God force. Of course in the West we regarded the idea with scorn – until the New Age arrived with its channellers and spirit guides and a new outbreak of Satanism. But all over the world and all down the centuries people have recognized the reality of these malign powers, and still do. Certainly in the Gospels there is no beating about the bush. Jesus believed in Satan. He came, among other things, to destroy the work of the devil in people's lives. So we find him casting out these dark spiritual forces. It is a major strand in the Gospels, and this ministry of deliverance continues today in many parts of the world. I have seen it time and again in my own job as a clergyman.

The meaning of Jesus' death

We might think that this life, demonstrating the love of God to all and sundry, this life of teaching, healing, and mending broken lives, was the main part of what Jesus came to do. But we would be wrong, according to those Gospel writers. Each of them dedicates between a third and a half of their entire book to the last few days of Jesus' life. Have you ever encountered a biography like that? Of course not. But these are no mere biographies. The Gospel writers concentrated on what they saw as most important, and that was the death of Jesus. Why did he come to such an untimely death, in his thirties, when his ministry was at most three years old?

Well, in a sense, his death was inevitable. For one thing, his enormous popularity was rocking the stability of the fragile peace with Rome and was likely to bring down savage reprisals that would embroil the whole nation. For another, he was perceived to have taken on the whole fabric of Jewish religion, Jew though he was. The focal points of Jewish worship and identity were the temple with its sacrifices, the law with its scribal interpreters, the sabbath with its restrictions, and circumcision, the seal of belonging to the Jewish people. But Jesus put a massive question mark at the heart of all these prized indicators of the special nature of the Jews.

He told people the temple would be destroyed, and his body would be a timeless 'temple' which God would raise up after his death, and make the centre of spiritual worship. These were mysterious words, not understood until much later. They were also dangerous words, which were raised against him at his trial. They could be construed as either blasphemy or signifying magic, and both were capital offences.

There was also his attitude to the law. This was very embarrassing to fellow Jews. On the one hand he seemed more at home in the law than any of them were, but on the other he was strongly opposed to their literalistic interpretation of it. He made his own revolutionary additions to the sacred text, and was ruthless in his attacks on clerical dishonesty and hypocrisy.

What is more, he seemed to be very casual in his approach to the sabbath. He even healed people on the sabbath day, to the disgust of the religious experts who saw this as forbidden 'work'. On one occasion the experts tried to gather evidence against him while he was in the synagogue. They drew attention to a man with a withered hand and asked if it was lawful to heal on the sabbath. Jesus, as quick-witted as ever, responded before restoring the man's hand: 'If any of you has a sheep and it falls into a pit on the Sabbath, will you not take hold of it and lift it out? How much more valuable is a man than a sheep! Therefore it is lawful to do good on the Sabbath' (Matthew 12:11–12).

As for the circumcision issue, Jesus frequently kept company with the dregs of society, people with whom the pious would never dream of associating. It was his way of showing that God cared for bad characters as well as good. But it scandalized the Jewish clergy. Worse, he was known to have defiled himself by helping non-Jews, such as Romans, Samaritans, Syro-Phoenicians – the uncircumcised scum. God loves them too, of course, and Jesus was demonstrating it. But it was too much for the Jewish authorities to stomach. It was inevitable that he had to be eliminated.

Not only do the Gospel writers show Jesus' death as inevitable. Astonishingly, they make clear it was voluntary. He said that nobody would take his life from him. He would lay it down of his own free will. We read that he steadfastly set his face to go to Jerusalem, knowing what would await him there. Three times in his final journey to Jerusalem he told his followers that he was going to his death. When he was arrested on that dark night in the Garden of Gethsemane, he could have asked his followers to protect him. He did nothing of the sort. Indeed, when one of them drew his sword, Jesus told him to put it away and then healed the ear of an attacker which the sword had severed. At his trial he could have spoken in his defence. Instead he remained silent. Even when hanging on the cross, the Gospel writers are clear that he could have asked for God to rescue him, confident that he would receive instant and decisive divine aid. Instead, he determined to go through with it, although every nerve in his body shrieked in protest. There was something mysteriously voluntary about the death of Jesus.

But there is more. The Gospel writers are all clear that Jesus' death was vicarious. It was on behalf of human beings, to benefit them. By now they were convinced that Jesus was no ordinary man: he had brought God into their midst. And as he perished in agony on that barbaric Roman cross they came to recognize at least four things about his death.

First, it was an example of supreme love. Here was the good shepherd who laid down his life for the sheep. He had said, 'Greater love has no one than this, that he lay down his life for his friends' (John 15:13). He not only fulfilled this, he exceeded it. As the apostle Paul put it a little later, he died for those who were at enmity with God. 'God demonstrates his own love for us in this: While we were still sinners, Christ died for us' (Romans 5:8). Amazing love. He loved human beings so much that he was prepared to drink the cup of suffering to the dregs, to die in unspeakable agony, so that nobody would be able to point the finger at God and say, 'He doesn't understand.' He does understand; he has stood in our shoes. He suffered as nobody else had ever suffered, so his friends believed. The cross was the demonstration of supreme love.

Jesus' death was also a rescue from mortal danger. The human race is in dire peril not only from international, social, economic and ecological disasters, but from one more serious still – we are out of touch with God. And most of us want to keep it that way. He is a threat to our independence, a check on our pleasures, and a judge of our actions. So we distance ourselves from him. Of course we do. And when God sees the alienation we have chosen instead of closeness to him, he cannot remain indifferent. We are in the wrong, and he cannot pretend otherwise, and so the gap widens. Alive mentally and physically, we are spiritual corpses. We are out of touch with God so comprehensively that we do not even recognize the extent of our separation. We have wandered deep into the wasteland and we are perishing there. We desperately need someone to ransom us and set us free.

That is where the cross of Jesus comes in. He died there to bridge the gap between us and God, to end the hostility, to bring reconciliation in place of alienation. He took personal responsibility for the wrongs we have done. He burdened himself with the debts to God we could never pay, and before he gasped out his life he was able to cry in triumph, 'It is finished!' The debts were squared. The job was done. That is why Jesus called his death 'a ransom for many'. That is why he said, 'God so loved the world that he gave his one and only Son, that whoever believes in him shall not perish but have eternal life' (John 3:16).

The New Testament writers also saw the death of Jesus as a solution of complete fairness. For God has a problem with us. From the dawn of time humans have chosen to go their own way. We have been rebels against God, ungrateful and self-centred. You only have to watch the TV headlines, or open the daily paper, to see it on every side. Human sinfulness is the most empirically verifiable of all Christian teachings! Inevitably that causes a problem between God and us. How can a holy God have unholy people in his presence without compromising himself? That is the problem.

In the cross of Jesus I see a perfectly astonishing answer. God could be perfectly fair on the one hand and have people like us back in his company on the other. What he did is breathtaking in its boldness, unassailable in its justice, and earthshaking in its generosity. He took our place. He condemned the wickedness of human beings and took the condemnation in his own person. He faced up to the poison in human hearts and drank the bitter cup himself. He did not pretend that our debts to him were not astronomical. But he paid for them out of his own account, and it crushed him. He upheld the penalty we deserved – and then went and endured it himself. And because Jesus was human, it was a man standing in for the human race at the place of our greatest need. Because Jesus was God as well as human, the effect of what he has done is limitless.

As John, the close friend of Jesus put it, 'He is the atoning sacrifice for our sins, and not only for ours but also for the sins of the whole world' (1 John 2:2). That is remembered constantly by the worldwide church at every communion service – 'his body given for me', 'his blood shed for me'.

Finally, the death of Jesus is a pledge of our total acceptance. How can we be sure God will accept us? And why should he? The answer lies in the cross of Jesus. Because he carried my accusing load on that cross I will never have to carry it. Well could the apostle Paul exult, 'Therefore, there is now no condemnation for those who are in Christ Jesus' (Romans 8:1). The cross is the seal on the whole transaction. It is the marriage ring to guarantee the whole relationship. It is the adoption certificate into the family of God.

The sequel

But the Gospel writers could not leave it there. All their accounts are lit up by the conviction that this Jesus who was crucified did not remain in the tomb, but was raised from the dead and is alive again. This was a totally unprecedented claim. The Jews believed in resurrection, but not until the end of history. So the idea of Jesus being raised to life again after three days would have struck them as totally bizarre – and interestingly the Gospel accounts show initial disbelief in all those who saw the risen Jesus. It was the last thing they were expecting. They could scarcely credit it. But once convinced they went all over the ancient world with their message. They were prepared to face mockery, persecution and martyrdom. Nothing would make them change their minds. So what convinced them?

First, the tomb of Jesus was found to be empty on the first Easter morning, though the grave-clothes were still in place. Second, Christianity, however, is not all about an empty tomb, but about a living Jesus. And that is what his followers found him to be over the next six weeks, in a whole variety of different locations and situations.

This brings me to the third piece of evidence I regard as very significant – the transformation of the disciples. A band of sad, demoralized cowards was changed into a group of evangelists and potential martyrs for whom death held no terrors. As Pinchas Lapide, a Jewish scholar, has written, 'Without the resurrection there would have been no Christianity.' He goes further. 'When this scared, frightened band of apostles which was just about prepared to throw away everything and flee into Galilee in despair . . . could be suddenly changed into a confident missionary society convinced of salvation, then no vision or hallucination is sufficient to explain such a revolutionary transformation.'

There is a lot more that could be said. What turned Saul of Tarsus, the scourge of the Christians, into Paul, the most passionate evangelist there has ever been? The resurrection. What changed James, the half brother of Jesus, from a pronounced sceptic into the leader of the Jerusalem church? The resurrection. (We read, 'he appeared also to James'.) And what continues to change men and women from their selfish, often wicked lives into new people with a fresh power, a fresh motivation and a fresh joy? It is encounter, they would tell you, with the risen Jesus.

The implications of the resurrection are enormous. If it is true, it means there is a life after death. It vindicates Jesus' position as Son of God. It suggests that his power is available for his people, the power they came to call the Holy Spirit of God. It means that he is currently Lord of the universe. It means that the world has not seen the last of him. He will return for judgment at the end of history.

These convictions encapsulate the main beliefs Christians have always held about Jesus. They are repeated world wide in that summary of Christian belief, the ancient Apostles' Creed: 'I believe in God the Father Almighty, maker of heaven and earth. And in Jesus Christ his only begotten Son our Lord, who was conceived by the Holy Spirit, born of the virgin Mary, suffered under Pontius Pilate, was crucified, dead and buried. He descended into hell. The third day he rose again from the dead. He ascended into heaven, and sits at the right hand of God the Father Almighty. From thence he shall come to judge the living and the dead . . . '

It is no doubt foolhardy to attempt to summarize Christian belief about Jesus in just a few pages. But we have at least glanced at the main outlines of that portrait of Jesus which the church has always treasured. He was divine as well as human. His life of love and service was matchless. His death availed to put human beings back in touch with God, if they were willing for change. And his resurrection not only validated his person and his claims but was the catalyst in forming the new 'society of Jesus', the church. That resurrection also made available something of its power in the life of the church, and it gave assurance of unending life with Christ and his people after this life is over.

There have been many variations on this theme, both within and beyond the churches. Down the centuries there have been many attacks on the Christian story. But rarely until this generation has there been such sustained opposition and disbelief. So I have set the scene by sketching, in this chapter, the main outlines of the traditional Christian beliefs about Jesus before looking carefully at the reasons why many today find the Christian story incredible. That examination will occupy the chapters which follow.

2. 'SCHOLARS ARE DISCOVERING A VERY DIFFERENT JESUS'

Is the New Testament based on fabrications?

In his celebrated blockbuster, *The Da Vinci Code*, first published in 2003, a little known writer, Dan Brown, gained instant notoriety. His book has been translated into more than forty languages, has headed most of the best-seller lists in the world, and for a while, at least, was unquestionably the most popular novel in circulation. It is a superb thriller, but it has an interesting sub-plot which sets out to undermine the credibility of the New Testament, the divinity of Christ, and the authenticity of the church, particularly the Roman Catholic Church. Brown's chief protagonist in the book claims that that 'almost everything our fathers taught us about Christ is false', and that 'the New Testament is based on fabrications'.

In the light of what we shall see in chapters four to six this would be a hard thesis to maintain if Brown did not come up with some alternative theory based on good evidence. Well, he comes up with an alternative theory all right, namely that there were earlier gospels giving a radically different picture of Jesus. These were suppressed when the canon of scripture was finalized in the fourth century, in favour of the 'less reliable' Matthew, Mark, Luke and John which, nevertheless, commended themselves to church authorities.

We will examine this thesis in due course. But first, why should we bother about the views of a novelist? Why not just enjoy the story? Partly because Brown's thesis will simply not hold water – and truth is always worth salvaging. Partly because the popularity of the book has meant there is a widespread assumption that the story recorded in the Gospels is at best doubtful and in all probability false. And partly because Brown's book does not stand alone.

Although there are only a tiny handful of scholars who share anything resembling his views, a positive rash of books and films has emerged based on these alternative gospels which Brown claims rubbish the story we find in the four Gospels. For centuries we have relied on the picture of Jesus presented by the four Gospels. But since 1945 it has been possible to maintain that there were several alternative gospels in circulation among the early Christians, and that they are, arguably, as reliable as anything we find in the New Testament.

What is the new evidence? – the Gnostic gospels

What, apart from the end of the Second World War, was so special about the year 1945? It was the accidental discovery of a large earthenware jar in the sands of Egypt near Nag Hammadi. Inside were thirteen old leather-bound books which can be dated towards the end of the fourth century AD. So this discovery was immensely important. It brings to light books that have been unseen for over 1500 years. The contents of this little library are immensely varied.

We have five non-canonical Gospels, namely the *Gospel of Thomas, of Philip, of Truth, of the Egyptians* and *of Mary*. There is a *Treatise on the Resurrection*, a supposed *Prayer of Paul*, strange stuff like *The Exegesis of the Soul*, the *Dialogue of the Saviour*, two *Apocalypses of James*, a bit of Plato's *Republic*, and the *Three Steles of Seth*. They are all now translated, edited, and published as *The Nag Hammadi Library* by the American scholar James Robinson. They turn out to have one distinctive feature in common. They are all Gnostic or

Encratite (ascetic) in character. There is not a single orthodox Christian work among the fifty-two contained in these volumes.

How did they get there? It seems likely that what happened was this. The jar of books was buried not long before AD 400. Maybe it was the treasured library of one of the Gnostic monasteries, hidden for protection. In AD 367 the Bishop of Alexandria, Athanasius, wrote a letter to the churches of Egypt defining the contents of the Christian canon of scripture with great clarity, and insisting that heretical books should not be read. It is all too possible that Gnostic monks, who were doubtless fond of their collection, hid them away in the sands and waited for a more liberal regime to emerge in due course! We do not know for sure. We do know that these pages were made of papyrus and written in Coptic – but the Coptic shows clear signs of having been translated, sometimes very inaccurately or with large gaps, from Greek originals, which will have been a good deal earlier. For example, it gives a full text of the *Gospel of Thomas* of which we previously had only a few fragments in Greek, written at the end of the second century.

It is these alternative gospels, massively at odds with what we read in the New Testament, which form the basis of revisionist pictures of Jesus, so beloved by the popularists like Dan Brown in his *Da Vinci Code*, or Michael Baigent, Richard Leigh and Henry Lincoln in their book *Holy Blood, Holy Grail*, or Margaret Starbird in *The Woman with the Alabaster Jar: Mary Magdalene and the Holy Grail*. And though these novelists and quasi-historians are no scholars, and show little first-hand acquaintance with the Gnostic gospels, as they are called, they rely on the few genuine New Testament scholars like professors Elaine Pagels and Karen King, who prefer the Gnostic to the canonical picture of Jesus.

Who were the Gnostics?

But it is high time to ask, who were the Gnostics? The answer is complex and hotly disputed. Nobody really knows the origin of Gnosticism, though it clearly emerged from fringe Judaism and Christianity, with input from Egypt and Iran, and even some obligations to Plato! It emerges in its full colours only in the second century AD, when it is seen in sharp conflict with orthodox Christianity. The word 'gnostic' comes from the Greek word *gnosis*, and indicates that the central element in it was a certain sort of 'knowledge'. Although there were many streams in this river of Gnosticism, some elements seem to have been constant. Here is a rough summary of them.

The first was a dualistic view of the universe. There was a supreme God, dwelling in unapproachable splendour in a spiritual world. He had no dealings with this world of matter. But there was a stream of emanations from this supreme God, becoming more and more crass until they resulted in the (evil) Demiurge, or 'world maker', who created the material world as we know it.

Second, Gnostics believed this world was evil, and human beings were imprisoned within it. They were incapable of ascending to the spiritual God. They needed a redeemer. The rescue or salvation was not from sin, but from bondage to matter, and from ignorance of our human plight.

Third, Gnosticism taught that some human beings (naturally, themselves!) were, fortunately, inhabited by a divine spark. This offered hope of escape from their corporeal existence. But there was nothing automatic about this, because even those who had the divine spark needed *gnosis*, knowledge. Faith was for the multitudes, knowledge for the few. And these few needed to be awakened to their plight and the possibility of rescue. The job of enlightenment and rescue was, in most of the Gnostic systems, the work of a divine redeemer who descended from the spiritual world in human disguise and was often, but not always, identified with the Christian Jesus.

Fourth, the human body was a tomb, and salvation was seen as rescue from that material tomb at death into a purely spiritual existence, to be reunited with the divinity from which a person's 'divine spark' had come. Of course, this disregard for the body opened up the way for two very different responses. It either produced asceticism, the way of the Encratites, which most Gnostics seemed to have chosen (the attempt to mortify the flesh so that the soul might more readily be saved), or else libertinism (which was based on the assumption that nothing a person did with his body could possibly affect the heavenly destiny of his soul). A minority of Gnostics, the Carpocratians and the Valentinians, were accused by the church fathers of choosing the latter option, and were soundly berated for it!

Fifth, Gnosticism embraced a highly-developed mythology full of archons, aeons and the like to span the gap between a good spiritual god and an evil physical world. Without the Christian element it is hard to see how Gnosticism could have entered into such intense conflict with the church. Without the mythological element it is hard to see how it could have become so popular.

Finally, we see in Gnosticism a doctrine, developed ultimately from Plato, which taught the immortality of the soul when released from the confines of the body. This, needless to say, was promised only to the elite, those who had *gnosis*. Here again there was a debt to Plato, who had virtually identified goodness with knowledge. We are miles away from the Hebrew conviction of embodied existence, both in this life and the next.

There was far more to Gnosticism than this. The church leader Irenaeus observed towards the end of the second century that there were almost as many systems of redemption as there were teachers of these mystical doctrines. But the outline is clear enough, both from the critiques offered by the church fathers, and from the Gnostic material itself which has turned up at Nag Hammadi. The Gnostics offered a very serious challenge to orthodox Christianity in the second and third centuries.

Two other aspects of Gnosticism are noteworthy. The first is its attitude to the Old Testament. Most Gnostics were strongly anti-Semitic and rejected the Old Testament as the product of the inferior deity, the Demiurge. The true spiritual God could not sully his hands by creating matter. But the orthodox could not tolerate this rejection for one moment. The God who redeemed mankind was the same God who brought humanity into being and grieved over his fall. So the Old Testament was properly a Christian book. The second aspect of Gnosticism that needs a mention is its attitude to women. The issue arises sharply in one of the earlier Gnostic documents that has come down to us, the *Gospel of Thomas*. Saying 114 concludes the document and reads:

> Simon Peter said to them 'Let Mary leave us, for women are not worthy of life.' Jesus said 'I myself shall lead her in order to make her male, so that she too may become a living spirit resembling you males. For every woman who will make herself male will enter into the kingdom of heaven.'

This seems a shocker, but attitudes to women were very different in antiquity from our own. The woman was the imperfect sex, because of the lack of a penis, and because their voices did not drop; nor did they grow a beard! Now the *Gospel of Thomas* assumes that all spirits will return to the place of their origin, where there will be no up and down, no male and female. But for this to happen women must first become male. The secret knowledge that Jesus offers Mary and those who like her 'make themselves male' is that by understanding his teaching they will enter the kingdom. I find it remarkable that radical feminists like Karen King and Elaine Pagels are drawn to this Gnostic material, which is so anti-feminine and offers nothing to substantiate their cause!

Gnostic and Christian beliefs contrasted

There are certainly some big contrasts between orthodox Christianity and Gnosticism. Gnosticism was a theosophy run wild – a view of divine wisdom in humans – and stood in striking contrast to the uniform teaching of the New Testament documents. In Gnosticism we are saved not from sin, but from ignorance. Not by a historical figure, but by a mythological one. Not by a Christ who is both divine and human, but by a divine Christ who only seems to be human (a view which is called Docetism, from the Greek word *dokein*, to 'seem' or 'appear'). Not by Christ's death and resurrection, but by understanding and assimilating the secret knowledge that Jesus purports to offer to the elect. Salvation not for all who sincerely repent and believe, but for a superior coterie of 'know-alls'. Not emancipation of the whole person but of the soul alone.

A taste of some Gnostic material

In the light of what we have seen about the Gnostic teaching, let us now look in a little greater detail at a few of these 'gospels' which have been discovered at Nag Hammadi, and see what they have to say about Jesus.

The Gospel of Thomas

This is the most important of the finds. But remember that it is not a gospel at all! It has no theme, no actions of Jesus, no crucifixion, no resurrection. It is simply a collection of 114 sayings attributed to Jesus. More than half of them show varying degrees of similarity to sayings in our Gospels. A few are almost identical. Others start like our Gospels but continue in a strange way. One such is Saying 2: 'Jesus said, Let him who seeks continue until he finds. When he finds he will be troubled. When he becomes troubled he will be astonished, and he will rule over the All.' The 'All' is a Gnostic idea and evokes a lot of comment in the Nag Hammadi writings. There are many Gnostic references in the *Gospel of Thomas*. The reference to 'the heaven above the heavens' (Saying 11) suggests a Gnostic cosmogony. 'I disclose my mysteries to those who are worthy of my mysteries' (Saying 62) betrays typical Gnostic arrogance so markedly different from the biblical teaching that none of us is worthy. 'Jesus the wise philosopher' (Saying 13) shows no interest in history of any kind. Jesus 'the revealer' comes up with a good deal of Gnostic thought and regularly sees the world as drunk or asleep. Jesus in Saying 28 says, 'I took my place in the midst of the world and I appeared to them in the flesh. I found them all intoxicated.' Here we have clear reference to the Gnostic Redeemer myth, whose function is to awaken the drunken or sleepy to the light that is already there within them. For 'within a person of light there is light and he lights up the whole world' (Saying 24). How different that is from the way Jesus speaks in John's Gospel.

Elaine Pagels, one of the scholars who has the greatest sympathy with the outlook of *Thomas* (she herself is a self-confessed Gnostic) is honest enough to contrast *Thomas* with John. '*Thomas's* Jesus directs each disciple to discover the light within ("within a person of light there is light") but John's Jesus declares instead that "I am the light of the world" and that "whoever does not come to me walks in darkness." In *Thomas* Jesus reveals to the disciples that "you are from the kingdom and to it you shall return" and teaches them to say for themselves that "we come from the light". But John's Jesus speaks as the only one who comes "from above" and so has rightful priority over everyone else.'

What is the date of the *Gospel of Thomas*? Some scholars opt for a very early date, despite the lateness of the text in which it appears. Some members of the sceptical Jesus Seminar, like Dominic Crossan and Stevan Davies, go so far as to date it between AD 50–70 and think it was in existence before our Gospels. Even those who would not go that far, like Elaine Pagels, are inclined to date it in the first century. Such a date would, of course, be very attractive to those who want to read Gnosticism back into the Christianity of the first century.

This early date, however, is increasingly seen as indefensible. For one thing *Thomas* knows and cites too much of the New Testament for such an early date. For another, distinctive Syriac forms of the text appear in *Thomas* – and the Syrians did not have the Gospels in their own language until Tatian produced his *Diatessaron*, around AD 160.

Tatian was the pupil of the Christian philosopher Justin Martyr, and created the *Diatessaron* (literally 'through the four') as a harmony of the four Gospels in Syriac, turning them into one continuous narrative. This was very popular in Syria and became the standard Gospel text there until the fifth century. In this blend of the Gospel material Tatian created some new forms of expression, and it is these which appear in *Thomas*. What is more, Thomas is called Judas Thomas in this gospel, and that name is found only among Syrian Christians.

Syriac scholars have also noticed that although the 114 sayings in *Thomas* seem to have no rhyme or reason about their sequence in Coptic or the underlying Greek, as soon as you translate them into Syriac you discover many catchwords which link almost all the 114 sayings in order to aid memorization. All of this adds up to the strong probability that *Thomas* was written towards the end of the second century.

If the *Gospel of Thomas* has nothing fresh and authentic with which to enrich our picture of Jesus, but only a second-century Gnostic rehash of material we find in the canonical Gospels, what about the other newly discovered gospels?

The Gospel of Peter

You see how desperate revisionists are for something to substantiate their case when Dominic Crossan writes a book, *The Cross that Spoke*, about the so-called *Gospel of Peter*, and dates it to around AD 50. The church fathers were aware of it, and as early as AD 200 condemned it as a forgery, but we had no copy of it until 1886. Then a substantial fragment of it was found in the tomb of a Christian monk who lived in the ninth century AD!

It is a garbled account of the passion of Christ, shows clear dependence on all four of our Gospels with the addition of extraneous material, hovers on the edge of Gnosticism, and has incredible mythological features like the stone on the tomb of Jesus rolling away under its own steam, two angels with heads reaching to heaven escorting a third figure out of the tomb, whose head reached higher than the heaven! And to cap it all, the cross follows them out of the tomb and speaks. You have to be pretty determined if you are going to argue that this is a true account of what happened!

The Gospels of Philip and Mary

Let's try one or two more, like the *Gospel of Philip* and the *Gospel of Mary*. Notice that the canonical Gospels are anonymous. Everyone knew that they recorded what Jesus taught so it did not matter very much who wrote them. But when you get the second-century so-called gospels teaching stuff that did not sound like Jesus at all, then they needed to make it sound credible by attaching apostolic names like Peter, Mary, Thomas and so forth. There is general agreement that the gospels attributed in this way to Philip and Mary come from the middle of the second century or later, are Gnostic in flavour, and historically worthless.

The *Gospel of Philip* is full of bizarre material, speaks of 'a man-eating God', the world that came into being by mistake, 'the mystery of the bridal chamber' and so forth. It would not have come into the public's notice at all were it not for Dan Brown's quotation from it about Mary Magdalene in the *Da Vinci Code*. He spins it for his own purposes, but the Coptic text itself is obscure and full of gaps.

Something similar occurs in the fragmentary document known as the *Gospel of Mary*. The text is in disarray and it does not even have a title – let alone the name of Mary in it. The Coptic version recovered from Nag Hammadi is late fourth century, but part of the text is found in a single page of Greek papyrus from the third century – and they do not even match!

It is about Mary Magdalene and her special vision of the ascent of the soul through the various heavens until it achieves its goal, final rest. A very Gnostic theme. It concerns secret knowledge, which Peter asks her to reveal (see page 54). She does – at length! When she has finished, Andrew and Peter are sceptical because what she has said is at odds with what Jesus taught them. Mary weeps because they do not believe her. Levi then takes her side, rebukes Peter, and exhorts the disciples to 'put on the perfect man' (that is, the perfect divine spark, beloved by the Gnostics) and proclaim the gospel throughout the world, 'setting no boundary or any further laws, as the Saviour said'.

This last looks like a Gnostic reaction against the regulations set out in Paul's pastoral letters about who may preach, be a bishop, and similar. You can well imagine a Gnostic woman who wants to teach, and is not allowed to do so by her bishop. The *Gospel of Mary* solves the problem for her by saying Jesus told Mary in a revelation not to lay down rules! We shall have more to say about these two references to Mary Magdalene in the next chapter.

The Gospel of Judas

In April 2006 the *National Geographic* magazine publicized what some sensationally called the most important biblical find for sixty years. It was the long-lost *Gospel of Judas*. Irenaeus had referred to it towards the end of the second century as 'fictitious history' but we did not know its contents until a fourth-century copy of it in Coptic emerged (in obscure circumstances) from the sands of Egypt. It is quite explicitly Gnostic, and represents both Jesus and Judas as enlightened Gnostic beings. Judas is Jesus' favourite and understands him as none of the other disciples do. 'Step away from the others, and I shall tell you the mysteries of the kingdom,' says Jesus.

The most notable thing about the lost gospel is the different motivation it gives for Judas' part in the arrest and death of Jesus. It is not a betrayal, as represented in the four canonical Gospels. Instead, it is all part of a pre-concerted plan between Jesus and Judas by which Judas is to be the agent in Jesus' capture and death so that his mission could be accomplished and his soul could be released from the prison of his earthly body.

'You will be cursed for generations,' Jesus says to Judas in the text, but 'you will exceed all of them, for you will sacrifice the man that clothes me.' The soul is released from the prison of the disreputable mortal body, to sail up to the spiritual God. And you can't get more Gnostic than that!

The *Gospel of Judas* tells us nothing of historical value about Jesus – it was written more than a century after his death. But it does shed some light on one of the Gnostic sects in the middle of the second century. They were the Cainites, who loved to reverse everything that was generally accepted, and identify with the villains in the biblical story, like Cain, Esau and the Sodomites. Judas would fit well into such company, so it is not surprising that they created this gospel *of* Judas (that is, about Judas) as opposed to the canonical Gospels which are 'according to' their authors.

But the stir which this publication produced in the American media was very revealing. It showed how Gnosticism's concern for the god imprisoned within you resonated with the current climate in the USA. Be true to the real you! How different that is from commitment to the kingdom of God. It is worth reflecting that material like the *Gospel of Judas* disappeared not because, as Dan Brown graphically put it, 'history is written by the winners' but because the Gnostic texts rejected the continuity between the Creator and the Redeemer, between Christianity and Judaism. Real Christians are called to be faithful to the God of Abraham, the God of Jesus – not to the god within them!

It is typical of Western attitudes these days to be very chary of commitment, whether in marriage or religion. We would rather believe we know the truth than check it out for reliability. Most people know quite well that the Gospel story is reliable, but do not want to commit themselves to following the one of whom it speaks: it is too costly. Therefore it is congenial to find an ancient text which reads the Jesus and Judas story back to front. It reinforces our prejudices and enables us to grasp at any excuse for not making a commitment to the truth.

The Secret Gospel of Mark

Let's end this examination of bogus claims to find a more reliable and different picture of Jesus than the one given in the Gospels, by looking at the most scandalous forgery of them all, perpetrated as late as 1960 by a scholar called Morton Smith. He announced that he had made a remarkable discovery in the desert monastery of Mar Saba near Jerusalem. In the back of a book published in 1646, on some blank pages, he says he found a letter, written in Greek and purporting to come from the second-century Christian leader, Clement of Alexandria. It quoted from a 'mystic' gospel of Mark, which was apparently read in circles of initiates in Alexandria. It describes Jesus raising a young man from the dead, and then the youth comes to spend the night with Jesus, 'his naked body clothed only in a linen cloth' so that he could be taught 'the mystery of the kingdom of God'. The homosexual allusion is hard to miss.

Morton Smith has gone to town on this. He wrote a massive book on it for scholars (mostly padding) and a short popular version called *Jesus the Magician*. He argued that Jesus was a homosexual, and this of course has been manna from heaven for film makers and scandalmongers. In addition Smith suggested another titivating element, a magical baptismal ceremony. Some members of the sceptical Jesus Seminar, largely composed of scholars on the fringe of New Testament studies, accepted the supposed letter of Clement as genuine and agreed it could point to an earlier version of Mark, superior to the one in our New Testament.

You would think that a claim like Smith's would bring the whole New Testament establishment running to examine the text for themselves. But no. The book in which Smith claimed to have found Clement's letter has totally disappeared! However he claimed to have photographed the letter, and these photos were closely examined by a lawyer and biblical scholar, Stephen Carlson. At the end of an exhaustive examination of all the facts, the conclusion he came to is clear from the title of the book he wrote in 2005: *The Gospel Hoax: Morton Smith's Invention of Secret Mark*.

It seems almost certain that Smith's theory of a 'Secret Gospel of Mark' is a gigantic hoax, and no less certain that he is the hoaxer! It is astonishing to find fraud of this immensity in scholarly circles, but perhaps we have some clues as to the reason. Morton Smith was an Episcopalian priest who had turned atheist. He was a celebrated practical joker. He loved provoking the faithful by his writings. Smith was himself a homosexual, and back in the 1950s that was a secret that needed to be closely guarded. We know that he was denied tenure at Brown University where he started his career, and he may have wanted to boost his standing by pulling off a coup of this nature. At all events, there are no grounds for claiming that allusions in the *Secret Gospel of Mark* correspond to anything in the life and teaching of the real Jesus. It is sheer moonshine.

Neither Morton Smith nor any of the others who claim to have discovered new and more reliable evidence about Jesus than what we read in the Gospels have been able to validate their claims. The solid, reliable evidence about Jesus is contained in the earliest records that have come down to us, the four Gospels.

So do these Gnostic gospels at which we have looked give us reliable new material about Jesus?

We have to conclude that they do not. In the first place they are not Gospels at all. A 'Gospel' tells the good news of God coming to our rescue with a real incarnation, a life of ministry and service, of teaching and love, before a terrible death and a glorious resurrection. These so-called gospels are not like that. They do not show any interest in the birth, ministry or teaching of the incarnate Jesus. They merely concentrate on putting into his mouth, after the resurrection, mysterious teaching which he could not possibly have given.

Second, they are all much later than the New Testament. Even the most sceptical scholars agree that our Gospels could not have been written later than the final quarter of the first century. None of the 'new' gospels was written as soon as that. The earliest may well have been the *Gospel of Thomas* but this shows evidence of knowing all four canonical Gospels and is therefore later than them.

Third, most of these newly discovered documents or their fragments (because practically none of them is complete) show evidence of the Gnosticism we have been examining, which was absent in the first century. Our New Testament writers show no knowledge of it because it was, as a system, not in existence in their day. It was a later corruption of Christianity by admixture with theosophical speculation. We must never forget that Christianity emerged from Judaism and not from the speculations of the Hellenistic world. These new documents show no knowledge of the Jewish background. In fact they are strongly anti-Semitic, and they regard the Old Testament, if they mention it at all, as the product not of God but of the evil Demiurge.

Were alternative versions of Christianity acceptable?

There is one other issue that needs to be addressed. Does the Gnostic material which has been unearthed, together with what we already know about the Ebionites (a branch of Jewish Christianity which stressed the humanity of Jesus and was less than confident of his divinity) mean that there were varieties of Christianity in the second century, all of which were acceptable in the church at large? Could you pick and choose what you believed about Jesus? Did it matter? That idea again would be a gross anachronism, although it is embraced by a few academics like Helmut Koestler and James Robinson.

To be sure, there were plenty of disagreements in the early Christian community – Gentile admission, meat offered to idols and the like. But the Christian mainstream was very clear that neither Docetism (which made Jesus so divine that he only seemed to be human) nor Ebionism (which made Jesus so human that he could not be divine) was acceptable. Nor for one moment did they tolerate Gnosticism's idea of secret revelations to an elite bunch. The Christian mystery was an open mystery, and all, not some, had access to it. There wasn't one Christianity which thought of Jesus as the Messiah and another that did not. There was not one Christianity that thought he died on the cross and another that did not. There was not one Christianity which held to a bodily resurrection of Jesus and another that had no time for it.

The trouble with those few scholars in the Jesus Seminar and others who think like that is that, as Prof. Craig Evans puts it, they are 'trying to smuggle into the first century a mystical, Gnostic understanding of God and the Christian life, even though the first century Christians had never heard of these things. The core message of Christianity, that Jesus is the Messiah, he's God's Son, he fulfils the scriptures, he died on the cross and thereby saved humanity, he rose from the dead – those core issues were not open for discussion. If you didn't buy that, you weren't a Christian.'

3. 'JESUS HAD A FLING WITH MARY MAGDALENE'

It is an astonishing phenomenon. The culture is awash with Mary Magdalene! Books about her pour from the presses: *Holy Blood, Holy Grail, The Jesus Scroll, The Woman with the Alabaster Jar, Bloodline of the Holy Grail, The Hidden Lineage of Jesus Revealed, Secrets of Mary Magdalene, The Secret Mary Magdalene, The Da Vinci Code, The Passion of Mary Magdalene, Magdalen Rising* and so on. Several of these have become films, and Channel 4 television has done more than one programme on her; and of course there is Abel Ferra's *Mary, The Last Temptation of the Christ*, and *The Da Vinci Code* film. In music there is Andrew Lloyd Webber's *Jesus Christ Superstar*, Richard Shindell's 'The ballad of Mary Magdalene', Johnny Cash's 'If Jesus ever loved a woman' and 'Lights of Magdala', to mention but a few.

If we ask why this rash of books, songs and films should have arisen at this particular point in history, the answer is complex. It is partly the arrival of feminism, and if it can be pushed back to Jesus' affirmation of Mary Magdalene, making her a major leader in his church, then that is a great scoop for the feminist cause. Partly it is the attraction of mystery: why should this woman be so prominently mentioned in the New Testament, and even more so in the Gnostic texts a couple of hundred years later? What lies behind it? Then there is our love of conspiracy theories, and where better than to find one here? What if Jesus and Mary had a liaison, or got married, or had a child? And it was all hushed up by the Catholic Church so that only now has it come to light? And there is more than a little iconoclasm about it – for if there was a conspiracy, that is a good stick to beat the Roman Catholic Church with: it has kept the secret all these centuries. But perhaps as much as anything we want to pull Jesus down to our level and make him normal, married, a lover, a parent, rather than this Son of God status the church has so long emphasized.

At all events there is a vast body of literature now which argues that Jesus was sexually linked with Mary Magdalene, perhaps married, and maybe they had children. It has even been suggested that they spawned the Merovingian kings of France! So it is time to examine the evidence with a critical eye.

What do we know of Mary Magdalene?

First, her name was not Mary but Miriam. This was an extremely common woman's name among Jewish women in the first century, and for that reason some distinguishing mark was often added to the name. In her case it was 'Magdalene'. This was not a surname at all, as we might imagine. It meant that she came from Magdala, which was a small fishing town on the west coast of the Sea of Galilee, an area where we know Jesus spent much of his ministry.

There must have been a time in her life when she was desperate. We are told in Luke (chapter 8) that Jesus cast out no less than seven demons from her. That indication of multiple possession may be a precise number, or, since seven is a perfect number in Hebrew thought, it may simply mean that she was completely set free. At all events, Jesus was very well known and in some circles much criticized for being an exorcist.

In gratitude for what he had done for her, Mary threw in her lot with him, and became one of the group of disciples, both male and female, who travelled the countryside with him. This in itself was most unusual. It illustrates his inclusive attitude towards women. Rabbis did not have women as well as men in their entourage, but Jesus did. There was no gender discrimination with him. Luke mentions Mary in this passage (Luke 8:1–3) as one of a group of women who not only travelled with him but helped him financially in his ministry. On any showing, she was very closely associated with Jesus.

We next hear of Mary at the cross. All four Gospels record that she was there at the crucifixion (Matthew 27:55f.; Mark 15:40f.; Luke 23:55; John 19:25), along with the other women. All four tell us that she was the first to encounter the risen Jesus on Easter morning (Matthew 28:1ff.; Mark 16:1ff.; Luke 24:10; John 20:1ff.). In every instance she is part of a small group of women disciples. In every instance she is named first.

John's Gospel gives an extended account of their Easter meeting. She wanted to cling on to him, still regard him as the prophetic teacher with whom she had travelled so much. But Jesus tells her that those days are over: he is about to return to the Father. Until his ascension it will not be possible for all his followers, wherever they are in the world, to have equal access to him. After that it will. She must prepare to relate to him in this new way, the way of faith rather than sight.

Mary had gone with some of the other women friends of Jesus to give a full anointing to the body of Jesus which had been hurriedly buried with some spices on Good Friday. But when it was plain that the body of Jesus was not there, but that Jesus had risen from the grave, she went with the other women to tell the apostles. But the claim was so stupendous that 'they did not believe the women, because their words seemed to them like nonsense' (Luke 24:11). So Peter went to the tomb to check it out for himself.

We do not know for sure if she was the same Mary, from Bethany, who anointed Jesus' feet with precious ointment before his arrest, and wiped them with her hair (John 12:3–7). Nor do we know if she was the unnamed woman penitent whose deep sin (prostitution?) had been forgiven and who, in gratitude, burst in on a supper party and anointed his head (Luke 7:37–50). This identification is very unlikely, and was only made in the sixth century AD by Pope Gregory I, but is rejected by the *Catholic Encyclopaedia* and most scholars today.

At all events, Mary of Magdala was one of the closest and most celebrated of all Jesus' followers. She is mentioned no less than twelve times in the Gospels. She was present in the ministry, at the cross and at the resurrection. The Eastern Church calls her 'the apostle to the apostles' because she and the other women were charged by Jesus to give them the first news of his resurrection (Mark 16:7). It is an accurate, if somewhat surprising description. For Mary was in the proper sense of the word, an apostle ('sent one') to the disciples. And that is how the Church Father Hippolytus, writing early in the third century, sees her. He tells how Christ showed himself to the (male) apostles and said to them, 'It is I who appeared to these women and I wanted to send them to you as apostles.'

Hippolytus rightly affirmed Mary and her women colleagues in their role as first witnesses to the resurrection, but neither she nor they were ever given any official leadership position in the church. The mistake of Professor Karen King and other ardent feminists is to impose a twenty-first century concept on ancient documents. Jesus did value women enormously, and he valued men too. But he did not espouse the restrictive cause of a fully fledged feminist, nor did he appoint women apostles.

That is all we know about Mary Magdalene from the earliest texts about her, the twelve references in the New Testament. What became of her we do not know. According to some late traditions she accompanied the apostle John to Ephesus where he married her, and in due course she died and was buried. An eleventh-century tradition spuriously claims that she evangelized Provence in France and lived in a cave in the Alps!

However, scarcity of information did not stop a lot of Gnostic speculation about her in the second and third centuries. We shall turn to it in a minute. But there is a prior question to examine.

Was Jesus ever married?

Many of the popular books about Jesus and Mary claim that they were lovers or got married. The question is, what evidence is there for this?

Let us be clear that there is no earthly reason why he should not have been married. It would not have imperilled his nature or his mission. But there is not a shred of evidence anywhere that Jesus was married!

It is argued by some that it was un-Jewish to remain unmarried, and that therefore Jesus must have been. But that will not hold water because the Essenes, a sectarian but much respected group within first-century Judaism, were all unmarried. Others argue that he was married, on the grounds of a couple of late Gnostic texts which we have looked at in chapter two, and will revisit below. They tell that Jesus kissed Mary and that the disciples were jealous of his special relationship with her. But even if we take these Gnostic texts as accurate, they give no suggestion of marriage or any sexual relationship between Mary and Jesus. There is, frankly, no evidence whatsoever that

Jesus was ever married, let alone to Mary Magdalene. It is sheer romantic imagination on the part of songwriters, film makers, and popular writers.

As is clear from Matthew 19:2–12, Jesus held a very high view of marriage. It is the Creator's plan for humankind, and divorce is wrong. But even in that passage he honoured those who had 'made themselves eunuchs', that is to say refrained from marriage, for the kingdom of heaven's sake. That is what he did himself. We read of his mother and family, brothers and sisters, but never of his wife. During his ministry, we read of his women disciples, but never of a wife. When he was tried and crucified, other women friends are said to be present, but there is no hint of a wife. After his death and resurrection his mother and family members are mentioned, but never a wife. Christians have no axe to grind in maintaining that Jesus was single. That is simply what the evidence makes clear.

What were the Gnostic gospels trying to do?

The *Gospel of Philip*, which we mentioned in the last chapter, appears to be a collection of excerpts from other Gnostic works, and was probably compiled early in the third century. It is certainly much later than the New Testament, from which it makes numerous quotations. Most people would never have heard of it, were it not for Dan Brown's advocacy of it in *The Da Vinci Code*. The way Brown presents it is as follows :

> And the companion of the Saviour is Mary Magdalene. Christ loved her more than all the disciples and used to kiss her often on her mouth. The rest of the disciples were offended by it and expressed disapproval. They said to him, 'Why do you love her more than all of us?'

However we have only one copy of this text, and it is full of gaps. It actually reads:

> And the companion of the [. . .] Mary Magdalene. [. . .] her more than [. . .] the disciples [. . .] kiss her [. . .] on her [. . .]. The rest of [. . .]. They said to him, 'Why do you love her more than all of us?'

As you can see, Brown is assuming a good deal in his reconstruction! From this sketchy allusion the novelist assumes that Jesus had sex with Mary Magdalene, and that the word 'companion' meant spouse. It does not. It means what it says, 'companion', and of course the passage says nothing about sexual union, only kissing. And kissing was very normal and a-sexual in first century Palestine, just as it is in many countries today (see 1 Corinthians 16:20; 1 Peter 5:14). The Coptic text is full of gaps, and does not reveal where Jesus is said to have kissed her. Even if it was on her lips that would mean little. There is another Gnostic text found at Nag Hammadi, the *Second Apocalypse of James*, which describes the risen Jesus imparting his mysteries to James by kissing him on the mouth and calling him 'my beloved'. It was a symbolic, non-sexual act.

But we can probably go further. There is another passage about kissing in the *Gospel of Philip*. We read, 'for it is by a kiss that the perfect conceive and give birth. For this reason we also kiss one another. We receive conception from the grace which is in one another.' This is very Gnostic. Professor Ben Witherington makes the point well. 'The aim of such kissing is spiritual birth or rebirth. Genital sex is avoided but holy kisses are allowed because what really matters is spiritual reproduction, not fleshly reproduction. The context of this material is clearly ascetic, which is in keeping with Gnostic literature in general.'

In any case, a document like this, full of palpable fantasy (read it and see for yourself!), can have no historical evidence to offer us about what happened nearly two hundred years earlier!

The other passage to which Brown and many others have recourse who make the most of Mary Magdalene, comes in the so-called *Gospel of Mary Magdalene*, though her name does not occur in the title. We looked at the passage in the last chapter. The Gnostic 'Mary' claims to have had special revelations from Jesus. Peter asks her to revel this secret knowledge: 'Sister, we know that the Saviour loved you more than the rest of women. Tell us the words of the Saviour which you remember but . . . which we have not heard.' Mary does so. When she has finished Andrew is very sceptical: 'I do not believe that the Saviour said this. For certainly these teachings are strange ideas.' Peter's view is the same. 'Did he really speak privately with a woman without our knowledge and not openly? Are we to turn around and all listen to her? Did he prefer her to us?' Mary weeps, and Levi jumps to her aid, rebukes Peter and encourages them all to get on with spreading the gospel (of the 'perfect man', that is, the divine spark in the true Gnostic's breast!). From this Brown draws the conclusion that it was not Peter to whom Christ gave directions to found the church. It was Mary Magdalene.

The idea is laughable, a novelist's liberty. There is nothing here about founding the church, only about the purported secret revelations on which the Gnostics thrived: they regularly attributed them to various characters who appear in the New Testament such as Judas, Philip and others. Nor is there any suggestion in the first century writings, which have come down to us in the New Testament, that Jesus gave pre-eminence in his church to a woman. In keeping with the social structures of the day, not to mention God's original design (Genesis 2), Jesus appointed the Twelve, all men, as his core group and Peter as their main spokesman and representative. Why this role for Peter? Because it was Peter who confessed that Jesus was the Son of God, and on Peter and his confession Jesus was able to build his church (Matthew 16:18). It was Peter, not Mary, who was given the keys of the kingdom. It was Peter, not Mary, who preached the first sermon at Pentecost. It was Peter, not Mary, who was called to authenticate the coming of the Holy Spirit to the Samaritans, and launch the Gentile church in the house of Cornelius.

While you will not find any scholars backing Dan Brown's flights of fancy, these passages in the *Gospel of Philip* and the *Gospel of Mary* have encouraged a minority of scholars, particularly Elaine Pagels and Karen King, to read back their feminist convictions into the early church. They see Mary Magdalene as the champion of female leadership. King writes that 'the apostles were considered to be guarantors of the true teaching of the church, and male bishops continued to be their sole legitimate successors. This male model of discipleship also provided (and continues to provide) a rationale for the exclusion of women from leadership roles, ignoring the presence of women disciples through Jesus' ministry, and as first witnesses of the resurrection.'

Professor King has an important point, but it is not the point at issue in the *Gospel of Mary*. It is shamefully true that women have not been given their proper place in the Christian church. It has all too often been run like a male club. And for that men need to repent and ensure that women do have proper access to leadership. After all it was the women who provided from their substance for Jesus during his ministry. It was the women who were the last to leave the cross and were the first witnesses of the resurrection. The church down the ages has robbed them of dignity and opportunities. Professor King is right to be indignant about it.

But the *Gospel of Philip* and *Gospel of Mary* are not, as Dan Brown thinks, about eroticism: nor, as Karen King thinks, about feminism (a glaring anachronism). They are concerned with something even more fundamental – rival views on the source of divine revelation. Gnostics who argued for secret esoteric revelations saw themselves as the downtrodden female (Mary) being abused by the hot-tempered male (Peter). It was a struggle about the true meaning of Christianity. Was its content determined by the New Testament scriptures to which the Catholic Church appealed, or by the secret revelations to which the Gnostics laid claim? And it is that momentous issue which makes the *Gospel of Philip* and the *Gospel of Mary* worth reading.

Did Jesus have homosexual partners?

Ours is a pansexual age. After all, if you reject the supernatural, as most of our Western world does, all you are left with is this world. And the most intriguing, mysterious and satisfying thing in this world is sexuality. It is hardly surprising that we are sex mad and that pornography has reached epic proportions. So single people are suspect. They must have some secret sex life. The idea of a godly person refraining from sexual activity is almost incomprehensible. So I am not at all surprised to hear that people are accusing Jesus of homosexuality. On what grounds? Because of the phrase, 'the disciple whom Jesus loved', referring to the young disciple, John. It must, they say, have a sexual edge. If he didn't have a fling with Mary Magdalene, why not with John?

To this we can offer a fairly trenchant response. First, there is no suggestion either in the New Testament or in subsequent history that Jesus had any homosexual attachment, just as there is no suggestion he was ever married. Certainly, Jesus is said to have loved John (as in John 21:7), but he loved Martha, her sister and Lazarus too (John 11:5). The same word is used in both contexts. Indeed it is the same word we find in the great commandment to 'love the Lord your God, and your neighbour as yourself' (Luke 10:27). It is the same word that occurs in the famous verse, 'God so loved the world that he gave his one and only Son' (John 3:16). It is the same word that shamed Simon Peter when Jesus asked him, 'Do you love me more than these?' There is no way you can read anything sexual into *agapao*, the word used for 'love' in all these cases. There is an entirely different word for sexual love in Greek, *eros*.

Moreover homosexuality was totally taboo in Judaism, which is why it is not ever so much as mentioned by Jesus. The Jewish law code in the Mishnah punishes it by stoning. It was seen as a Gentile vice and as such is condemned strongly by the apostle Paul for both males and females at the end of chapter 1 of Romans. Again in 1 Corinthians 6:9 we are told that both active (*arsenokoitai*) and passive (*malakoi*) male homosexuals, along with thieves, adulterers and swindlers, will not inherit the kingdom of God. So strong was this revulsion from the very start of the church that Christians, along with Stoics, were responsible for changing the whole climate about homosexual liaisons. These had been viewed tolerantly and even enthusiastically in the Roman world, but were outlawed once the empire adopted Christianity. They were seen as an unworthy expression of the sexual energies God had given for marriage and the procreation of children. To imagine that Jesus himself was a homosexual, given his first-century Jewish context, is, quite simply, ludicrous.

4. 'JESUS? HE'S JUST A MYTH'

When I was working in Canada some years ago, Tom Harpur, a journalist and broadcaster (and formerly an Anglican priest) who had taken leave of Christianity, could be relied on to attack the faith he once believed whenever opportunity offered. In 2004 he went further and wrote a book, *The Pagan Christ*, in which he claimed that 'there is nothing the Jesus of the Gospels either said or did . . . that cannot be shown to have originated thousands of years before, in Egyptian mystery rites and other sacred liturgies'. In other words, Christianity was a sort of copycat religion. Its account of Jesus is worthless.

You find something similar in a book jointly authored by Timothy Freke and Peter Gandy. They ask in *The Jesus Mysteries*: 'Why should we consider the stories of Osiris, Dionysus, Adonis, Mithras, and other Pagan Mystery saviours as fables, yet come across essentially the same story told in a Jewish context and believe it to be the biography of a carpenter from Nazareth?' Again, 'the story of Jesus and the teachings he gives in the New Testament are prefigured by the myths and teachings of the ancient Pagan mysteries. Each mystery religion taught its own version of the myth of the dying and rising Godman, who was known by different names in different places. In Egypt, where the mysteries began, he was Osiris, In Greece he becomes Dionysus, in Asia Minor he is known as Attis, in Syria he is Adonis. In Persia he is Mithras, in Alexandria he is Serapis, to name a few.' The writers conclude that 'Christianity was a heretical product of paganism'.

Robert Price, another ex-Christian, is an engaging sceptical writer in the Jesus Seminar, whom I had the pleasure of debating in 2007 in the University of Florida. He argued that

Christianity represents the coming together of several currents in ancient religion. The dying and rising Saviour, whose salvation you receive by faith and sacraments, 'is a mutation of the Osiris or Dionysus religion'. At some point, he believes, it was combined with 'a form of oriental Gnosticism whose advocates preached an Inner Christ'. To this was added myths and legends about the Divine Hero, widely celebrated in the ancient world. And it was all topped off with episodes rewritten from the Old Testament. Eventually Jesus was imagined to have been a historical figure. Dr Price allows that Jesus just might have existed, but regards it as questionable. He even suggests Christianity might have started as a hoax!

Was Christianity derived from pagan myths?

Whilst Dr Price's doubts whether Jesus ever existed are extreme, even within the Jesus Seminar, the idea that Christianity borrowed heavily from pagan myths has been around for a long time. The early Christian Fathers in the second century were well aware of the similarities between the story of Jesus and some of the ancient pagan myths. But the idea of a copycat religion really arose in Germany at the end of the nineteenth and the start of the twentieth century. It was put forward by the 'History of Religions' school. It was popularized by Sir James Frazer in Britain when he published his readable, but unreliable, The Golden Bough in 1906 – the first book in English to compare Christianity to the mystery religions. He discussed Isis and Osiris, Attis and Mithras and suggested that we should look to these 'mystery religions', as they were called, for the origins of Christianity.

This seemed an attractive hypothesis for a while, but subsequent scholarship has examined this hypothesis and found it wanting, for a number of reasons. Nowadays it is regarded as a dead issue by almost all scholars. Other academics went in for somewhat similar syncretistic ideas, and believed the Christian story was influenced by a wandering miracle worker like Apollonius of Tyana or the Gnostics – who all lived after Jesus and so were unable to oblige as sources!

What were these mystery religions which are supposed to have been the cradle of Christianity? They grew out of the age-old fertility cults and nature worship. People were fascinated by the successive rise, flowering, fall and rebirth of the seasons of the year. At the heart of the mystery religions was the longing for new life. And as sex is intimately connected with new life, some of the mystery religions went in for sexual obscenities. But this was incidental to the purpose of the worshippers. They were looking for divine aid to enrich their lives here and now and perhaps offer them the hope of immortality afterwards.

There were many different mystery religions, but they all held out to their initiates the hope of a better life, and deliverance from an oppressive and capricious Fate, which could quench your life at a moment's notice, and condemn you to unspeakable horror after death. They were secret societies, had a great sense of community, and enjoyed special initiation rites and fellowship meals.

Fascinating as these mystery cults were, they remain obscure, because the initiates were forbidden to tell what went on in them. Leaks were few and far between. There are plenty of theories, but there is not much to go on. We can say with confidence that the earliest of them was the ancient Eleusinian mysteries, celebrated in Greece in honour of Demeter, the corn goddess, from at least the seventh century BC. But towards the end of the first century BC various Eastern cults became popular as the Orient became part of the Roman world, and copied the Greek practice of mystery initiations. The Egyptian deities of Isis and Osiris were particularly popular, and we have two partial descriptions of the cult dating from the second century AD – without divulging its secrets!

The mysteries flourished as belief in the old gods of Greece and Rome waned. The world was a dangerous place, and a century of civil wars had preceded the start of the Christian era. There was a widespread hunger for security, significance and meaning. People turned to the mysteries in their search for spiritual support, for a close fellowship, for a special status, and for hope of immortality. They had, like Christianity, a concern for salvation, but that salvation was rescue from Fate and (usually) from the terrors of the afterlife, not from sin.

It is a mistake to lump these various mystery religions together. They had their own characteristics. Some of their stories and rituals do have parallels with particular aspects of Christianity, such as initiation rites and a sacred meal, but as we shall see, the contrasts were far greater.

The crucial difference between Christianity and pagan myths

The essential difference between Christianity and the mystery religions was really quite simple. It lay in the person of Jesus of Nazareth. Demeter, Osiris, Dionysus and the rest were all mythical figures. Nobody believed they had actually lived. They were legendary, mythological figures, invented to explain some of the aspects of life, sexuality and death. In striking contrast, however, Jesus was a recent and well-attested historical figure. Lots of people actually knew this man whose life, death and resurrection made such an impact. This point is absolutely crucial and sets Jesus apart from all the mythological saviour figures of the mystery cults, and indeed from the founders of other religions.

A faith like Buddhism or Confucianism could survive even if it were proved that Buddha or Confucius never lived. It is their teaching which is important. But that is not the case with Christianity. It is not primarily a system of religious rituals and ethics. It is basically good news about a unique historical person, who died a mere thirty years or so before the Gospels began to appear. Lots of eyewitnesses were still alive who could have checked their accounts. If you could disprove the historicity of Jesus, Christianity would collapse like a pack of cards. For it all depends on the conviction that a historical person, Jesus of Nazareth, shared God's nature as well as our own. And that is a matter not of ideology or mythology but of history. We are faced, then, with two questions. First, did Jesus ever live? And second, even if he did, are the stories we have of him drawn from – or at least influenced by – the mystery religions? First, then,

Did Jesus ever live?

Christian evidence

The most important evidence we have is the four Gospels. Written between AD 60 and 85 as the eyewitness generation was beginning to age and die, they embody the oral proclamation of previous decades, and as we have seen, they represent an entirely new form of literature. They are not so much biographies or histories: they are 'good news' about this Jesus. Needless to say, with so much at stake, they have been under repeated attack, but today their stock stands as high as ever. I wonder when you last read one? You do not need to approach them as inspired scripture in the first instance: merely as the attempts of honest contemporaries to bear testimony to the person, death and resurrection of the most significant person the world has ever seen, the man who split history in two. There is, after all, no other great man who can boast of a third of the human race worshipping him two millennia after his death!

Well, you may say, their evidence must be prejudiced. We cannot believe the Gospels. Very well, let's begin by looking at some of the secular evidence for the historicity of Jesus. Four non-Christian authors, writing within seventy years of his death, tell us something about him.

Roman evidence

Tacitus, the greatest historian of the Empire, who wrote towards the end of the first century AD, tells us that Jesus was the founder of the Christian faith, and that he was crucified under Pontius Pilate, who governed the turbulent little province of Judea from AD 26–36. His followers had so increased by 64 AD when the Great Fire of Rome broke out, that Nero tried to blame them for starting it, covered them with pitch, and set them alight in his gardens. Tacitus did not believe this for a moment and thoroughly disapproved of Nero's brutality, though he scorned the Christian 'foreign superstition'. Read all about it in his *Annals* 15.44:

> Nero fastened the guilt and inflicted the most exquisite tortures on a class hated for their abominations, called Christians by the populace. Christus, from whom the name had its origin, suffered the extreme penalty during the reign of Tiberius at the hands of one of our procurators, Pontius Pilatus, and a most mischievous superstition, thus checked for the moment, again broke out not only in Judaea, the first source of the evil, but even in Rome, where all things hideous and shameful from every part of the world find their centre and become popular.

Then there was Thallus, who in around AD 52 completed a history of the world from the Trojan War to his own day. Amazingly, he included a reference to the darkness which the evangelists say engulfed the land at the death of Christ (Mark 15:33). This fragment survives, though most of the rest of Thallus' work is lost. It is cited by Julius Africanus about AD 220 and reads: 'Thallus, in the third book of his *Histories*, explains away this darkness as an eclipse of the sun – unreasonably, as it seems to me' (because a solar eclipse cannot take place at full moon, and it was at the season of the paschal full moon that Jesus died). But this piece about the darkness at the cross, which Thallus thought important enough to include in a history of the whole world, shows two things very clearly. First, that the story of Christ's passion was known in Rome in non-Christian circles by around the middle of the first century. And second, that the enemies of Christianity tried to give it a naturalistic interpretation.

Suetonius, a Roman court historian who around AD 125 wrote up the lives of the first twelve Caesars, also mentions the cruel treatment of Christians after the Great Fire, but his most interesting comment comes in his *Life of Claudius* 25: 'As the Jews were making constant disturbances at the instigation of Chrestus, he [the emperor Claudius, who ruled from AD 41–54] expelled them from Rome.' Clearly Suetonius found a record of Jews quarrelling over one Chrestus (a variant spelling in Gentile circles of Christus) and inferred – wrongly – that this person was actually in Rome at the time of Claudius. Almost certainly the dispute reflects tensions in the Jewish ghetto as debates about Christ made their impact. And that indicates that there were substantial numbers of Christians in Rome in the forties of the first century! That is to say, only a decade or so after the death of Jesus. After all, some Romans were present in Jerusalem on the Day of Pentecost, weeks after his death (Acts 2:10).

Pliny the Younger was a wealthy man of letters who climbed the traditional Roman ladder for top people, and in AD 112 became governor of the province of Bithynia in north-west Turkey. When he arrived there he came across lots of Christians, and wrote to the Emperor Trajan asking advice on what to do about them (*Letters* 10.96). The whole, rather extensive letter is fascinating, particularly the sentence, 'They were in the habit of meeting on a certain fixed day [that is, Sunday] before it was light, and they sang hymns to Christ as God and bound themselves by a solemn oath [*sacramentum*] not to commit any wicked deed, but to abstain from all fraud, theft and adultery . . . ' From his investigations of the movement, Pliny was left in no doubt about Jesus as a recent historical figure whom vast numbers of people worshipped.

Jewish evidence

Perhaps the most interesting of all these non-Christian testimonies comes from the pen of Josephus. He was one of the Jewish commanders in the war against Rome, and after AD 70 he set out to re-establish the credit of Judaism in the minds of Roman society in general and the imperial family (his patrons!) in particular. This he did between AD 75 and 95 by writing an important series of books, the *Antiquities of the Jews* and the *Jewish War*. There is a remarkable passage in the *Antiquities* 18.3.3:

> And there arose about this time [Pilate's time] Jesus, a wise man, if we should call him a man; for he was the doer of marvellous deeds, a teacher of men who receive the truth with pleasure. He led away many Jews, and also many

Greeks. This man was the Messiah. And when Pilate had condemned him to the cross on his impeachment by the chief men among us, those who had loved him at the first did not cease; for he appeared to them on the third day alive again, the divine prophets having spoken these and thousands of wonderful things about him: and even now the tribe of Christians, so named after him, has not yet died out.

This is, of course, a most surprising testimony to find in the pages of a Jewish writer. Josephus was certainly no Christian. But all attempts to impugn its genuineness are special pleading and can be said to have failed. It has as good attestation as anything in Josephus. It is included in all the manuscripts. The early Fathers knew it – the fourth-century historian Eusebius quotes it twice. Probably some of it is sarcastic: 'if indeed we should call him a man' may refer to his divine claims, and 'this man was the Messiah' to the charge affixed to his cross, while the passage about the resurrection may merely be reflecting Christian propaganda. Be that as it may, we have in Josephus a powerful independent testimony to the historical reality of Jesus of Nazareth. The stories about Jesus were no myth. They were so circumstantial and so well attested that they found a place in the apologetic work of the Jewish Josephus, who had the strongest possible reasons for keeping quiet about anything so inconvenient to his theme.

It is not surprising in the light of this evidence that, as Otto Best put it, 'no serious scholar has ventured to postulate the non-historicity of Jesus'. Even James Frazer, whose *The Golden Bough* sought the origins of Christianity in the mystery religions, as we saw, concluded, 'The doubts which have been cast on the historical reality of Jesus are, in my judgment, unworthy of serious attention.' But, second, we must ask,

Did the mystery religions influence the story of Jesus?

The virgin birth?

Matthew, who was a close disciple of Jesus, and Luke, who tells us that he had carefully investigated everything about Jesus from the beginning, both report that Jesus was born of a human mother Mary, but had no human father. He was conceived through the intervention of God himself. This is, of course, highly improbable unless the Christian claim is true, that Jesus shared both God's nature and ours, in which case it is not only credible but makes perfect sense. Those who believe the mystery religions influenced the New Testament point to this conviction about Jesus' virgin conception as a prime example of Christian dependence on pagan sources.

The truth of the matter is that there is no parallel anywhere to the chaste, awesome story we find in the Gospels. Here we find no suggestion of intercourse between God and Mary, unlike all the pagan stories of the lustful amours of Zeus with mortal women. Plenty of these stories existed, and they were often designed to enhance the importance of the person thought to have been conceived in this way. You would find them inside the mystery religions and beyond. They go right back to Homer, and were great stories – which nobody took seriously. They certainly never attributed them to any historical person. Here are a couple of samples.

Orphism was one of the early Greek mystery cults. In the Orphic myth, Zeus, disguised as a serpent, had sex with Persephone, and Zagreus was born. However Hera, the jealous wife of Zeus, had Zagreus torn apart and devoured him. But Athena saved his heart – which Zeus swallowed, and thus was enabled to beget Dionysus. Persephone herself was later revered as a Corn Maiden goddess and also as wife of

Pluto, Lord of the Underworld. She spent four months with him below and then rejoined her mother, Demeter, the Corn Mother, for the remaining eight months of the year. Stories like these clearly had to do with the death and rebirth of the crops, but in due course (we do not know when, because all the relevant sources are late) the hope of human immortality came to be read into the rituals of the Orphic cult.

Here is another version of the myth. Dionysus, the god of wine and fertility, had his special Bacchanal mystery cult or 'orgies' celebrated by women alone, and some detractors of Christianity claim that his was a virgin birth. However that is not the case. Ovid and other ancient poets tell how Zeus, disguised as a human, had intercourse with a human girl, Semele. Needless to say Hera, Zeus' consort, got jealous. So Semele had to go. The deal was that she was struck with a thunderbolt, but her son was to be immortal. Zeus sewed the unborn child into his thigh until Dionysus was born! Another story tells of Zeus and the mortal girl Danae. Her father, warned by an oracle that Danae's son would kill him, shut her up in a bronze chamber. But Zeus visited and impregnated her there in a shower of gold. Her father, Acrisius, then put her and her baby, Perseus, in a chest and set it afloat.

All such stories are obviously mythological and provide more contrasts than comparisons with the virginal conception of Jesus. They were the result of lust, attributed by the Greeks and Romans to their gods, whom they saw as overgrown humans, complete with human vices. The Jewish and Christian concept of God has no such anthropomorphism and there is no suggestion either of lust or of intercourse in the birth stories of Jesus. The children of the liaisons of Zeus and other gods with mortal women were thought to be heroes, half human and half divine. The Christian understanding of Jesus is that he was both fully God and fully human. In all these pagan stories it is the lust of the god, rather than the absence of a human father, which is the centre of interest. Could anything be more remote from the story in Matthew and Luke than these myths of the lust of Zeus?

Sometimes we are told that Alexander the Great and Krishna and Buddha had virgin births, and that the claims for Jesus were derived from one of them. But this, too, will not bear examination. Alexander was unquestionably the child of Philip of Macedon and Olympias, a passionate and murderous woman who bore her husband Alexander and Cleopatra. The story of Alexander's conception from Zeus was put out later to enhance his stature when he was already the most important person in the world, and was demanding worship. Interestingly enough, it was strongly denied by Olympias! As for Buddha and Krishna, the sources we possess are no earlier than five hundred years after their deaths, so that does not inspire much confidence. According to the legend, Buddha's mother (no virgin, but married many years earlier) dreamed that he entered her womb as a white elephant (which must have been painful!), while Krishna was born not to a virgin at all, but to a mother who had seven previous sons.

It is apparent that none of these pagan stories is anything like the non-sexual virginal conception which lies at the heart of the account in Matthew and Luke. Raymond Brown, a distinguished New Testament scholar, concludes his examination of the evidence thus: 'No search for parallels has given us a truly satisfactory explanation of how early Christians happened upon the idea of a virginal conception, unless, of course, that is what really took place.'

The resurrection?

The 'History of Religions School' to which I referred earlier amassed a number of parallels between the death and resurrection of saviour gods in pagan mythology and the story of the resurrection of Jesus. They suggested that Christianity copied the pagan stories and attached them to Jesus. Did not Osiris, Attis and Mithras rise from the dead? If so, may not Christianity have historicized those stories and applied them to their hero, Jesus?

Attis was, in mythology, the youthful consort of the Mother Goddess Cybele, and the prototype of her eunuch devotees. It is an old story with many variants, but our main source comes from Pausanias who lived long after Christ, in the middle of the second century AD. Attis was driven to castrate himself and was killed by a wild boar. That is why the priests of Cybele were always eunuchs. The best Cybele could do was to preserve his dead body. In some versions of the myth his hair continued to grow, in others he returned as an ever-green tree. This was doubtless because he was seen as a god of vegetation, and his death and rebirth became a popular spring agricultural festival to celebrate the death and rebirth of the vegetation and crops, particularly after this oriental cult had been admitted to Rome by the emperor Claudius (AD 41–54). He had a fascination for curious religions! Of course, nobody imagined that Attis had ever existed, let alone had left an empty tomb and appeared to his followers over an extended period. His festival was all about getting good crops. And though we have four texts which speak of his 'resurrection' they date from between the mid-second and fourth century AD, were inspired by the cycle of the year, and could not possibly have influenced the Gospel account. Indeed, they were very probably influenced by the Christian claim of Jesus' resurrection.

Osiris was Egyptian, and represented the dead Pharoah. He died and had a new existence as Lord of the Underworld. Once again, there are several accounts, of which the most widely known was this. He was killed by his brother, and chopped up into fourteen parts. The goddess Isis felt sorry for him and tried to collect and reconstitute the parts. She could only find thirteen – and Osiris was buried. He does not come back to this world, but remains in the Underworld. He appears with Isis in her mystery cult, which was widespread. Though details are obscure, their festivals became popular in the Empire, and according to Apuleius, himself an initiate in the middle of the second century AD, included initiation rites, processions, music and dances, a professional Egyptian priesthood and water from the Nile. Not much or a parallel to the resurrection of Jesus!

As for Mithras, he was very much the god of soldiers and merchants, and no women were involved in his cult. Mithraism became a popular mystery cult in the second century AD when it became a serious rival to Christianity. Its first mention is in a poem by Statius, around AD 90. Mithras was associated with light and the sun-god, and curiously he was said to have been born out of a rock. Mithraic temples were usually underground, where his capture of a bull was celebrated. We have no record of the death of Mithras, let alone of any resurrection! But one interesting feature in his worship was the occasional slaughter of a bull over a grating in the mithraeum, and an initiate under the grating was drenched in its blood. This was very rarely done until the late third century, when it seems to have become a regular part of the initiation of a new member. The famous inscription 'renatus in aeternum' ('born again for ever' – through the blood of the bull), which is often adduced as a parallel for Christian rebirth, is dated in the fourth century so could not possibly have influenced Christian belief. More probably Christianity had influenced Mithraism in their struggle for the souls of men.

Conclusion

Enough has been said to show that there is no validity in the claim that Christians drew their accounts of Jesus from the mystery religions. For one thing, the similarities are more specious than substantial. And where similarities do exist they do not necessitate dependence – that would be a major fallacy. For another, the mysteries belonged to the Graeco-Roman world, not the fiercely monotheistic Jewish society where Christianity was born. They were part of the hunger for security, significance and meaning in a dangerous world where the old Roman religious beliefs had collapsed. Their membership was exclusive and closely guarded. Any so-called resurrection they celebrated was cyclical like the year, not once-for-all like the resurrection of Jesus. What is more, not only the Jews but the earliest second-century Christian writers were passionately opposed to the mysteries, so it is most unconvincing to imagine that the first Christians drew from them.

The mysteries made no moral demands upon their initiates. In Christianity, however, membership demanded a change of life. Moreover, the mystery religions all failed, whereas Christianity went on to become the largest faith the world has ever seen. This would have been exceedingly improbable, if Christianity was simply one of the genre of mystery religions.

Detractors of Christianity, particularly in popularist books, often exaggerate the similarities and then use language borrowed from Christianity to describe pagan rituals. Often they get the chronology wrong and assume dependence when the mystery religion material in question is post-Christian.

Finally, the mysteries celebrated mythical heroes, whereas Christians worshipped a historical figure whom many of the earliest of them knew well, and who, on good historical evidence, to which we will turn in a later chapter, they believed to have risen uniquely from the clutches of death into the power of an endless life. In short, there is no mystery religion that asserts that the god dies and is raised from the dead in order to lead his faithful to eternal life. The analogies adduced are totally unconvincing. In the succinct words of Mircea Eliade, an important historian of religion, 'There is no reason to suppose that primitive Christianity was influenced by the Hellenistic mysteries.'

5. 'THE NEW TESTAMENT MANUSCRIPTS ARE UNRELIABLE'

Anyone who has done much in the way of commending the Christian faith to others will have faced objections such as these.

- 'Those Gospel stories were written at the end of the second century and are totally unreliable.'
- 'The text of the New Testament is so corrupt that we can't know what the original writers said – or meant.'
- 'The New Testament we have today is nothing like the original.'
- 'There are so many textual variants in the New Testament that we cannot believe what it says.'

If objections like these hold water, it will indeed be the case that we cannot know what Jesus was like or what he achieved: it will all be hidden in a fog of uncertainty.

There is another aspect of the problem that is increasingly brought forward as an Islamic presence advances in Western nations, particularly Britain. Muslims believe the Christian scriptures are corrupt, in strong contrast to the perfection of the Qur'an in Arabic where the text (at any rate as presented these days) has no variants.

All in all, there is a case to answer!

When were the New Testament documents written?

Our New Testament consists of twenty-seven books, namely four Gospels, a variety of letters, mostly by Paul, the Acts of the Apostles, a treatise to Hebrew Christians, and the Book of Revelation. In the years following their completion, there are references to nearly all of them in the Christian writings at the end of the first century such as 1 *Clement*, the *Epistle of Barnabas* and the *Didache* (or 'Teaching of the twelve apostles') and those at the start of the second century, such as Ignatius's and Polycarp's. The New Testament must therefore have been complete by the last quarter of the first century AD.

Jesus' ministry began, Luke tells us (3:1), 'in the fifteenth year of the reign of Tiberius Caesar', that is to say AD 27, and lasted for some three years. This means that he was almost certainly executed in AD 30. A great deal of work has been done on the dating of the New Testament writings which bear testimony to him. The broad consensus of scholars would date Paul's letters between AD 49 and 65. They are the earliest part of our New Testament, with the possible exception of the Letter of James, which may date from earlier in the forties. The Gospels emerge a little later. Most scholars put Mark's as the first, around AD 60 or 65, followed by Luke and Matthew in the seventies and John either before AD 70 or a decade or so later. The precise dates remain a hot topic of scholarly debate. The Acts was either written in the early sixties, which would entail an earlier date for Luke, since Acts is volume 2 by the same writer, or it may derive from the seventies. Hebrews was very probably written a little before AD 70 to encourage Christian Jews not to return to Judaism in the hour of its distress, with Roman armies camped around its walls. Revelation was probably written under the persecuting Emperor Domitian in the nineties. It is a fiery tract maintaining that Jesus, not the Emperor, is the Lord of the world.

At all events, there is no doubt that the Gospels were written in the first century. Nobody who has really examined the evidence can doubt that.

What are the dates of the earliest manuscripts we possess?

In the middle of the nineteenth century an influential school of thought based in Tübingen argued that the Gospels and Acts did not exist before the thirties of the second century. This theory was based not so much on historical evidence as on philosophical presuppositions derived from Hegel. Even then it was clear that the facts were otherwise, as Lightfoot and others ably demonstrated. Nowadays the evidence is far greater and more conclusive in favour of a first century date for the Gospels, no matter what our presuppositions may be. We are in a better position to assess the reliability of the text of the New Testament than we are with any other ancient document.

Take Thucydides, for example. He was the famous Greek historian who wrote the *History of the Peloponnesian War*, about 400 BC. The earliest manuscript we have of Thucydides dates from the tenth century AD. Yet no classical scholar of any stature has ever doubted that we have what Thucydides wrote, simply because of the thirteen-hundred-year time gap between his autograph edition and our earliest existing copy.

Or think of Tacitus, the distinguished Roman historian who wrote in the nineties of the first century AD. Books 1–6 of his *Annals* come from a single Latin manuscript of the ninth century AD. Books 11–16 come from a single eleventh-century manuscript. Yet nobody doubts that this is what Tacitus wrote. Because the issues are so great, it is only with Christianity that people take refuge in questioning the reliability of the textual tradition.

Now in striking contrast to this slender and late manuscript attestation to these great classical writers like Thucydides and Tacitus (and the situation is similar with others, such as Julius

Caesar, the earliest text of whose *Gallic War* dates from nine hundred years after his day) we have as many as five thousand Greek manuscripts of the New Testament in part or in whole. The best and most important of these are two famous codices, Sinaiticus in the British Museum and Vaticanus in the Vatican library. They date from about AD 350 and are beautifully and very carefully written. But in addition, and even more important, are considerable fragments of New Testament books, written on papyrus, which can be dated a lot earlier. The Chester Beatty Papyri were made public in 1931 and they include portions of eleven papyrus codices, three of which contained most of the New Testament. One of them, containing the Gospels and Acts, can be confidently dated to about AD 200, while the Bodmer Papyri, donated in 1955 and housed in Geneva, and containing most of the Gospels and Epistles, date from a little before AD 200.

There are no other ancient documents where the gap between the original composition and the first extant copies is as small as it is in the case of the New Testament. Moreover, the attestation comes in many languages (such as Coptic, Greek, Syriac and Latin) from different parts of the ancient world, and this provides an immensely reliable text for the New Testament.

Of course there are textual variants, because there was no printing and mostly amateur scribes wrote in response to dictation from the front of the room. Inevitably, therefore, we find variations, particularly as some vowels in Greek sound very much like others: just occasionally we are still not sure what is the correct reading. There is a famous example in Romans 5:1. Did Paul write, 'Therefore being justified by faith we have peace with God' or 'Therefore being justified by faith let us have peace with God'? The Greek words from which these variants come would have been pronounced identically!

However it is important to understand that no single doctrine of any sort in the New Testament depends on a disputed reading, and that in probably every case we have the original reading in one or other of those five thousand partial or whole manuscripts. Actually, the text is so certain that nobody dares to suggest conjectural emendations (that is, suggestions of what the text ought to read!), which are common among classical scholars. We can be confident that we have the Gospels as they were written. There are only two serious questions about the text. One is whether Mark 16:9–20 was written by the evangelist, or added a little later by another hand to a Gospel which otherwise seemed to end very abruptly at 16:8. The other is whether the story of the woman caught in adultery belongs in John 7:53 – 8:11 or after Luke 21:28, where some manuscripts place it.

Recent discoveries underline the solidity of the manuscript tradition yet further. It was not so long ago that even so distinguished a New Testament scholar as Rudolf Bultmann was disposed to date John's Gospel towards the end of the second century. So it is one of the ironies of fate that we now have an actual fragment of that Gospel, known as P52, which can be dated on stylistic grounds to between AD 100 and 125. This was found in Egypt and is now a prized possession of the John Rylands Library in Manchester. It was uncovered on a rubbish dump in a provincial town on the Nile, far removed from its traditional place of composition (Ephesus in Asia Minor) and proves conclusively that this, the latest of the four Gospels, must have been written well before that date. The text of P52, by the way, is identical with that of later manuscripts.

We may be able to go even further back, since we now have a small fragment of Mark's Gospel, chapter 6, found among the Dead Sea Scrolls which were hidden in the caves by the Dead Sea when the Romans came to 'settle the Jewish problem' in AD 66. We have in Oxford fragments of Matthew, chapter 26, which look on palaeographical grounds to have been written before AD 70, though this is disputed. There is a document known as *The Unknown Gospel* which was discovered a few decades ago. It is dated by the experts to between AD 100 and 150 and shows knowledge of all four Gospels, demonstrating that they were all written and reckoned to be authoritative well before that time. The fact that the unknown writer quotes from all four suggests that they may well have been bound together in a single volume by then. We know they were not long afterwards, when Tatian wrote his *Diatessaron*, a conflation of the four Gospels, and we actually have a copy of all four bound up with Acts in P45, one of the Chester Beatty Papyri to which we referred earlier. The early heretic Valentinus, whose *Gospel of Truth*, written in Rome about AD 140, has been discovered comparatively recently, quotes extensively from the New Testament writings that are in our Bible. Heretics knew they had to do this if they were to get a hearing for their new ideas.

So by AD 100, if not a little earlier – that is to say within the lifetime of some who had known Jesus – the New Testament was not only written but was on the way to being collected. Furthermore, from the outset it was regarded as authoritative – so authoritative that Christians began to quote it with the same reverence with which they quoted the Old Testament. So authoritative that the heretics knew they had to quote it if they were going to win a hearing for their heresy. Accordingly, you find the late Sir Frederic Kenyon, a very distinguished authority on ancient manuscripts, summing the matter up as follows:

> The interval, then, between the dates of the original
> composition and the earliest extant evidence becomes so

small as to be in fact negligible, and the last foundation for
any doubt that the Scriptures have come down to us
substantially as they were written has now been removed.
Both the authenticity and the general integrity of the New
Testament may be regarded as finally established.

What, then, of the Muslim claim that the biblical text is corrupted?

Anyone who has discussed Christianity with Muslims will have
come across the accusation that the biblical text is corrupt.
However, Islam is curiously self-contradictory on this matter.
On the one hand the Qur'an speaks of three tracts of scripture
that were revealed before Muhammad – the Law of Moses, the
Psalms and the Gospels (suras 3.93, 4.163, 5.46). Jews and Christians are called 'people of the book', and Muslims are told to
believe the previous scriptures as well as the Qur'an. 'Believe
in Allah and his messenger and the scripture which he revealed
previously' (sura 4.136). The Qur'an confirms the truth of that
which was revealed before it (35.31). But on the other hand
there are four verses in the Qur'an which accuse the Jews
of 'falsifying' or 'twisting the meaning' of the scriptures by
changing words from their context (2.75, 4.46, 5.13, 5.41). However none of these verses suggests that the text of the Bible is
corrupt, merely that certain Jews have been falsifying it. There
are only two verses in the Qur'an where similar accusations
are made against Christians. In 2.140, Christians are blamed for
concealing parts of what God has revealed in their scriptures,
and in 5.14 of forgetting part of that revelation. Neither of
these justifies the deep-seated Muslim conviction that the text
of the Bible is corrupt. Where then, did it come from?

The answer is instructive. The accusation that Christians
had tampered with the text of the scriptures first appeared in

an eleventh-century Muslim apologist, Al-Juwayni, and then became commonplace. He appears to have done so to explain the discrepancies between the Bible and the Qur'an. The most important of these were the sayings about the Paraclete in John's Gospel ('I will ask the Father, and he will give you another Counsellor to be with you for ever', John 14:16; cf. 14:26; 15:26; 16:7), which Muslims believe predicted the coming of Muhammad, while Christians denied the claim. For the record, Jesus never spoke of another prophet coming after him, and Muhammad was not with his followers for ever!

The Islamic position is very difficult to sustain. If they claim that the scriptures were corrupted before the time of Muhammad, why does the Qur'an say that the message revealed to Muhammad was a confirmation of the previous scriptures? 'He has revealed to thee [Muhammad] the scripture with truth, confirming that which was before it, even as he revealed the Torah and the Gospel' (3.3). But if they claim that the corruption of the text came after the time of Muhammad, they have to face the fact that the manuscripts on which our Bible is based were written centuries before Muhammad and the text in them is, as we have seen, reliably attested from many parts of the world. It would seem that the Muslim assault on the New Testament scriptures as corrupt is unsustainable.

Of course, part of the claim, at any rate nowadays, is based on recognition of the apparent contradictions and the textual variants in the Christian scriptures. Christian scholars have long been aware of these and seek to explain them in a variety of ways. But they seem utterly scandalous, and provide clear evidence of textual corruption to the Muslim mind, because of their very different view of scripture.

To the Muslim it is essential that scripture is perfect, revealed to the illiterate Muhammad by Allah in Arabic with no possibility of error. Christians hold that scripture is indeed God's revelation, but it comes in many forms through a whole variety of human authors, down several centuries. Muslims persist in comparing like with unlike, thinking that Christians place their scriptures in the same category as Muslims place the Qur'an. This is wrong. Muslims believe God's supreme revelation was given in a *book*. Christians believe it was given in a *person*, and the New Testament scriptures bear testimony to that person. The proper comparison is not between the Qur'an and the Bible, but between the Qur'an and Jesus. Christians have nothing to fear from such a comparison.

There is, I think, another reason why Muslims have latched on to this eleventh-century claim that the Gospels have been corrupted. It lies in their reliance on the *Gospel of Barnabas*. This is a document containing some of the stories in the four Gospels but with a strong Islamic slant. It is clearly written by a convert to Islam. The book is sheer propaganda – Jesus is not the Son of God, he was not crucified, he proclaims the future coming of Muhammad and so forth. It tells us Jesus said he was not the Messiah, and that Muhammad was, though both the New Testament and the Qur'an give that title to Jesus alone. The *Gospel of Barnabas* was of course never mentioned in the ancient world for the simple reason that then it did not exist.

Muhammad Ata ur-Rahim's attempt to find it attested in the early church confuses the *Gospel of Barnabas* with the late first century *Epistle of Barnabas*! The oldest manuscripts of the *Gospel of Barnabas* are in Spanish and Italian. It was probably written by a Spaniard of Jewish background, who had become a Muslim, and it was discovered in Amsterdam in 1709. There is no evidence of its existence before that time. It seems to be a rather clumsy forgery, full of historical and geographical errors, and images that seem to come from the fourteenth-century poet Dante, like 'circles of hell'. It breathes the atmosphere of the Middle Ages, not of the ancient East. The book is worthless and only deserves a mention because many modern Muslims seem to credit it and use it in their propaganda.

Of course, the underlying reason for Muslim belief that the scriptures are corrupt is that they speak of Jesus as the Son of God. Therefore they must by definition be corrupt. However, that is no way to treat an ancient text. The presence in a document of material unacceptable to later generations does not, of course, invalidate the authenticity of that text!

In short, the Muslim charge of corruption in New Testament texts carries no conviction, but could certainly be applied to the fictitious *Gospel of Barnabas* on which they appear to rely.

6. 'THE NEW TESTAMENT STORY IS INCREDIBLE'

We saw in chapter four that Jesus of Nazareth quite certainly was a historical figure and cannot be dissolved into a myth or a saviour figure, such as we find in one of the mystery cults. And in chapter five we saw not only that the attestation for the New Testament documents is far stronger than for any other ancient books, but that the gap between when the authors wrote and the earliest copies we have is so short that any idea of massive corruption of the text is untenable.

But that still leaves open an important question. Granted that we have the texts substantially as they were written, can we believe what they say? In particular can we believe that Jesus was as they portray him? There are plenty of people who find their content so improbable that they remain very sceptical about the Christian claims.

Can we trust the Gospel writers?

The notable thing that strikes us when we read the four Gospels is that the first three of them, Matthew, Mark and Luke, follow much the same pattern and give us a very similar view of Jesus, often in almost the same words. That is why they are called Synoptics. Mark is the shortest, and was clearly used as a source by Matthew and Luke. Indeed there are only 31 verses in Mark that have no parallel in Matthew or Luke. So the question is, can we trust Mark?

The Gospel of Mark
There is a very interesting comment in Eusebius' *Ecclesiastical*

History (3.39). After Luke, he was the first great historian of the church, and lived AD 269 to 339. He is quoting Papias, who was a bishop in Hierapolis shortly after AD 100 and wrote a five volume *Exposition of the Oracles of the Lord*, which has perished apart from quotations by later authors. And Papias tells us that he received this material from someone even closer to the apostolic circle than himself. He calls him 'the Elder'. You could hardly have better evidence than that.

> Mark, having been the interpreter of Peter, wrote down accurately all that he [Peter] mentioned, whether sayings or doings of Christ; not, however, in order. For he was neither a hearer nor a companion of the Lord; but afterwards, as I said, he accompanied Peter, who adapted his teachings to the needs of the hearers, not as though he was making a compilation of the sayings of the Lord. So then Mark made no mistake, writing down in this way some things as he [Peter] mentioned them; for he paid attention to this one thing, not to omit anything that he had heard nor to include any false statement among them.

Papias is saying that Mark's Gospel is largely dependent on Peter, a key disciple of Jesus. He claims that Mark, though not himself one of the apostles, was a close colleague of Peter, was careful to be accurate in recording what Peter preached, and that his gospel was not chronologically but more topically arranged.

New Testament scholars long suspected that behind Mark's record lie independent stories transmitted orally in the early church, joined together by historically valueless editorial glue in the shape of generalizing summaries. But modern study has shown that, far from being editorial inventions, these short summaries can be put together to give a rough outline of the story of Jesus' life. What is more, something very similar happens in the Acts of the Apostles (for example, 2:14ff.; 3:12ff.; 4:10ff.; 13:23–30; cf. 1 Corinthians 15:3ff.). This rough outline in Acts stretches from the preaching of John the Baptist to the resurrection of Jesus – and that turns out to be precisely the scope of the Gospel of Mark!

The stories in that Gospel are what a preacher would naturally use to fill out the historical outline. So Mark is an expression of the gospel story as it was related in the earliest days, and as preachers, particularly Peter, proclaimed it to the varied situations of his hearers. Mark 'the interpreter of Peter', will have been valuable in translating Peter's Aramaic into Greek, and there is no shortage of evidence in the Gospel that much of the material originally existed in the language of Jesus himself, Aramaic.

Mark's Gospel is almost universally acknowledged as the earliest, and emerged in the early sixties AD, a mere thirty years after the events it records. That is a small gap in the ancient world where, unlike ourselves, people valued the spoken word more than the written. In any case, it was hard and expensive to get hold of books. But as the first generation began to die off, it became imperative to set the record down and to do so accurately. That is what Mark set out to do. His Gospel is mainly about what Jesus did, rather than his teaching. That makes good sense. It is the person of Jesus, his death and resurrection, that he concentrates on, and that is exactly what the early preachers stressed – the death and resurrection of Jesus, and the importance of commitment to him.

The Gospels of Matthew and Luke

When people became Christians they obviously would have wanted to know more about the central figure they had come to trust, especially what he taught. And it is striking that the greater part of the material common to Matthew and Luke consists of sayings or teachings of Jesus. This has led to a widely held conjecture that another document as early or earlier than Mark existed, referred to as Q (the first letter of *Quelle*, German for 'source'). Matthew and Luke drew heavily on this source, which like Mark shows many signs of the Aramaic beneath the surface. It seems to have consisted entirely of the teaching of Jesus.

Matthew and Luke naturally each had their own outlook and purpose in writing their Gospels. Both of them expand Mark by the accounts they give of Jesus before his public ministry began and after the resurrection. Matthew's Gospel is clearly organized into five great sections, and may well have been designed as a handbook for Christian teachers in the early days just after AD 70, when the church became distinct from the synagogue down the street. Luke, for his part, wanted to set the story of Jesus within the framework of the secular history of the time (for example, 3:1ff.) and to recount it as part one of his two volume work. Dedicating the book to Theophilus, probably a wealthy Christian patron, he shows in his Gospel what God had begun to do in the work of Jesus and then, in the Acts of the Apostles, what God continued to do in the staggeringly speedy growth of the Christian faith throughout much of the ancient world.

We have another quotation from Papias, short and enigmatic, but highly significant. He tells us, 'Matthew compiled the Logia in the Hebrew [i.e Aramaic] tongue and everyone translated them as best he could.' While there have been many guesses as to what this might mean, it cannot refer to our Gospel of Matthew, which was written in Greek, not Aramaic. But it fits Q like a glove. Those sayings of Jesus would very likely be in Aramaic – indeed, as shorthand was well known in antiquity, they could well have been written down in the lifetime of Jesus. And Matthew collected these 'Logia', that is, 'sayings' or 'oracles', and put them out in their original Aramaic. And when Papias says that everyone translated them as best he could, he means that people made their own translations – and this may account for the slightly different form in which some of the Q material appears in Matthew and Luke.

Luke tells us that he was not an original disciple of Jesus but had thoroughly researched all the material (Luke 1:1–4). The interesting thing is that he was the companion of the apostle Paul, and thus very close to the heart of the action. For we must never forget that the letters of Paul were written before the Gospels, that is, between AD 48 and 64. This man had been a highly educated Jewish rabbi, passionate for Judaism, a persecutor of the new Christian sect – and yet he became not only a Christian but its most powerful advocate. It will have taken some very strong evidence to convince him. His letters are not written to record the life and ministry of Jesus. They were written to Christians who already knew it. Yet in those Pauline letters we can find enough allusions to reconstruct the gospel story of Jesus.

Paul insists on his divine pre-existence, but knows he was a real human being, a descendant of Abraham and David who lived under the Jewish law, was betrayed and on the night of his betrayal instituted a memorial meal of bread and wine. He endured the Roman penalty of crucifixion although the Jews were the ones responsible for his death. He was buried, rose from the grave the third day, and was thereafter seen by many witnesses, the vast majority of whom were still alive in the early fifties when Paul alludes to them in his first Letter to Corinth. Moreover, Paul knows the apostles of Jesus, of whom Peter and John are pillars of the Jerusalem community, and he knows James, the brother of Jesus. He is aware the apostles were married. He quotes Jesus on the subject of marriage and divorce and the words he used to institute the Lord's Supper.

There are many other allusions to the life and teaching of Jesus in the writings of Paul, but these are the most obvious ones and they come from one who was converted to Christianity only three or four years after the death of Jesus, and whose account of the gospel was the same as that of the original disciples.

Naturally Luke would have been privy to all this material. He was a close companion of Paul, acted as his doctor and endured prison with him. So what with Mark, Q and Paul, Luke had a lot to go on. He probably spent time in Palestine gaining material for his two-volume work during the two years that Paul was in prison before they set off together under guard to Rome. His two-volume work may well have emerged in the seventies, but quite possibly was published some years earlier, just before the death of Paul in AD 64. That is the most obvious occasion for the publication, since Luke ends his Acts leaving Paul in prison at Rome on appeal to the emperor, and it is hard to imagine the evangelist not telling us whether his friend had been executed or released.

Although the Acts of the Apostles relates events subsequent to the death of Jesus it is highly relevant to the question of the reliability of the evangelist. For Luke offers us a great deal of information about cities and officials in the Roman empire, which archaeology and classical studies have emphatically confirmed. He does not make a single mistake. If he can be so accurate where he can be checked, as in Acts, is it not reasonable to suppose he was just as careful in what he records in the Gospel, where he cannot be checked? So much, in brief, for the Synoptic tradition about Jesus. It is both early and reliable.

The Gospel of John

The Gospel of John presents a somewhat different picture. Although clearly showing us the same Jesus, there are many changes of emphasis in his account. For one thing Jesus is publicly revealed as Son of God right from the start. The chronology of events is sometimes different, and so is the way Jesus speaks – in theological discourses rather than the homely parables recorded by the Synoptics. This difference of atmosphere and detail in John has led to a great deal of discussion over the centuries. Let's see how it may bear on the issue of John's reliability.

It has long been persuasively argued that we can progressively zero in on the author of the Gospel. He was a Palestinian Jew, an eyewitness, one of the Twelve, one of the inner circle – along with Peter and James – and above all 'the disciple whom Jesus loved'. This disciple was present at the Last Supper, the crucifixion and the empty tomb on Easter morning (13:23; 19:26; 20:2ff.). It was he who wrote the Gospel. 'This is the disciple who testifies to these things and who wrote them down' (21:24). The external evidence, too, is strongly in support of John as the author. But if so, why is his Gospel so different from the Synoptics?

For one thing he records a phase of Jesus' ministry in the region of Judea prior to the imprisonment of John the Baptist. For another, his account of the ministry covers three years whereas the more topical arrangement of the Synoptics makes room for only one visit to Jerusalem – when he met his death. Surprisingly, he omits both the Lord's Prayer and the account of the institution of the Lord's Supper. But by the time he wrote, possibly well into the eighties AD, both of these were constantly in use in the churches, and did not need repetition. It is quite true that there is a lack of parables in the Fourth Gospel. But John concentrates on the Jerusalem scene and the theological disputes between Jesus and the religious leaders, rather than the agricultural hearers he would have had in Galilee, where homely parables were invaluable. As a matter of fact, the Synoptic Gospels bear occasional witness to his speaking in the style we find in John (for instance, Matthew 11:25–27). And in John 10 we find teaching about the Good Shepherd and his sheep which is strongly reminiscent of the Synoptic parables.

But the most important question, of course, is this. Does John represent the same Christ as the Synoptics do, or is there a major discrepancy between them? All the Gospels regard Jesus as the Son of God. When John speaks of him as the Word he is using language that would make profound sense to the diverse backgrounds of both the Jewish and Greek readers of his work, which was almost certainly written in a Greek context in Asia Minor (Turkey). To be sure, Jesus is revealed in all his splendour from the start of this Gospel, whereas the disciples only gradually became aware of it in the others. But this is readily understandable.

John had been meditating for decades on the person of the Jesus whom he had followed as a very young man, and whom he had long worshipped as Lord and Saviour. He saw every aspect of the story of Jesus he records in the light of its consummation at the resurrection. In his old age in Ephesus he realized that the context of Jesus' ministry in Palestine had passed away beyond recall, especially with the destruction of Jerusalem, and he wanted to make plain to his readers the eternal validity of that life, death and resurrection. So he set himself to organize his book in a way that would communicate clearly with men and women who were quite unfamiliar with its original setting. Yet in so doing, he was careful to avoid telling the story in such a way as would compromise its uniqueness. And he succeeded brilliantly.

Although his Gospel is the most profound of the four, it is the one which seems to most effectively draw enquirers into Christian commitment. John introduces us to Jesus as God's final revelation, as love incarnate, as the one whose life really is the light of human beings. Countless people have pondered on the seven signs he gives as to who Jesus is, and the supreme sign of the cross and resurrection, and have become his disciples. It was William Temple who put the matter so succinctly and so truly. 'The Synoptists may give us something more like the perfect photograph. St. John gives us the more perfect portrait . . . Let the Synoptists repeat for us as closely as they can the very words he spoke: but let St. John tune our ears to hear them.'

The problem of miracles

Can we believe them?

There is, however, another problem when considering the trustworthiness of the New Testament picture of Jesus: the miracles. It is widely assumed by the man in the street, and frequently among theologians, that miracles do not happen, and that therefore the Gospel story, which contains numerous miracles, cannot be relied upon for accurate information about Jesus. The miracles of Jesus must be repudiated, because miracles do not happen: so ran the message of a film, Who was Jesus? And such a view seems very reasonable. After all, how can we in the twenty-first century be expected to believe in miracles? The trouble is that you simply cannot disentangle Jesus from the miracles attributed to him. Scholars in the nineteenth and twentieth centuries tried very hard to discover a non-miraculous Jesus. They utterly failed. Every strand of the Gospel material shows Jesus as someone who was endowed with different capabilities from other people.

The greatest miracles were his conception without human father, which we have already examined in chapter four, and his resurrection, to which we will turn in chapters eight and nine. Both raise massive questions, on which each of us needs to make a decision. But what about the plentiful miracles which are recorded in the Gospels throughout his ministry?

Of course, if we believe that the miracles of his conception and resurrection validate the claim that he brings God among us, that makes it much easier to accept the lesser miracles attributed to his ministry. But you may be still in the process of making up your mind about who Jesus is, and you find the miracles a stumbling block. After all, miracles don't seem to happen. But why should they not happen if God really did come into our world in the person of Jesus? The laws of nature do not necessarily forbid them. A 'law of nature' is simply the name we give to a series of observed uniformities. This is the way the world is. But if a contrary instance is well attested, scientists will widen their so-called law so as to include both the uniformities and the exception. In the case of Jesus there is a lot of contemporary evidence, from his friends and his opponents alike, that he was just such a 'contrary instance'.

C. S. Lewis is someone who reflected hard and long about miracles in the New Testament. His book *Miracles* is very illuminating on the subject. He makes it clear that a miracle does not break the laws of nature.

If God creates a miraculous spermatozoon in the body of a virgin, it does not proceed to break any laws. The laws at once take it over. Nature is ready. Pregnancy follows, according to all the normal laws, and nine months later a child is born. We see every day that physical nature is not in the least incommoded by the daily inrush of events from biological nature or from psychological nature. If events ever come from beyond Nature altogether, she will be no more incommoded by them. Be sure she will rush to the point where she is invaded, as the defensive forces rush to a cut in our finger, and there hasten to accommodate the newcomer. The moment it enters her realm it obeys all her laws. Miraculous wine will intoxicate, miraculous conception will lead to pregnancy, inspired books will suffer all the ordinary processes of textual corruption, miraculous bread will be digested. The divine art of miracle is not an art of suspending the pattern to which events conform, but of feeding new events into that pattern . . .

He adds that belief in miracle requires two conditions. 'First, we must believe in the stability of nature, which means that the data offered by our senses recur in regular patterns. Second we must believe in some reality beyond Nature.' Which is why he concludes that 'the mind which asks for a non-miraculous Christianity is a mind in process of relapsing from Christianity into mere "religion".'

And that is what the disciples found themselves unable to do. Compelled by the evidence of their own eyes, they were in no doubt about his miracles. And there is some fascinating supporting evidence for the miracles which is not as well known as it should be. It is a fragment of the first Christian apologist, Quadratus, who wrote early in the second century in an attempt to commend the truth of Christianity to the Roman emperor, Hadrian:

But the works of our Saviour were always present (for they were genuine); namely those that were healed and those who were raised from the dead. They were not only seen in the act of being healed or raised, but they remained always present. And not merely when the Saviour was on earth, but after his departure as well. They lived on for a considerable time, so much so that some of them have survived to our own day.

I find it intriguing that the only passage of Quadratus to have come down to us should bear testimony to this most improbable aspect of Jesus' life, his miracles. It shows how confidently the early Christians could count on the impact not only of what Jesus said but of what he did.

There are traces of his miracles in Roman and Jewish sources as well. The Gentile philosopher, Justin Martyr, writing his *Apology* about AD 150 can say with casual assurance, 'That he performed these miracles you may easily satisfy yourself from the *Acts* of Pontius Pilate.' Jewish leaders, likewise, are unable to deny the reality of the miracles of Jesus: they simply assign them to the power of Satan (Mark 3:22 and similar). In the Acts of the Apostles we find Jews attempting to use the name of Jesus as a potent spell in exorcism – with unfortunate consequences for themselves! (Acts 19:13ff.). Later on this continued, so much so that the rabbis had to forbid Jews from trying to heal in the name of Jesus. For the open minded person, willing to be convinced by sufficient evidence, the conclusion is compelling. Jesus exhibited miraculous powers, and not once or twice but habitually.

What do these miracles mean?

This raises the question, what do the miracles of Jesus mean? Are we supposed to be impressed by a series of conjuring tricks? They seem to me to mean at least five things.

At the most basic level, the miracles reveal a God who cares. He cares so much about the condition of poor, broken humanity that he comes in person to show himself as the doctor, the rescuer (see Mark 2:17). And wherever he goes he demonstrates that divine compassion. Often exhausted by his work, he is never once recorded as having sent anyone away unsatisfied. He cared. He healed.

Second, the miracles constitute a claim by Jesus as to who he really is. The miracles to do with nature are a good example of this. The Old Testament is clear that it is God who multiplies food and feeds the hungry. But on two occasions Jesus himself does this for thousands of people. The implicit claim is evident. Or think of Jesus walking on the water of the Sea of Galilee in a storm. Was this to show off? Not at all. It was to teach the terrified disciples a crucial lesson, that Jesus does what God does. In the Psalms we read that it is God who stills the raging of the sea. And what God does in the Old Testament Jesus does in the Gospels. The conclusion stares us in the face. Jesus embodies God and brings him into focus as nobody else has ever done. The miracles are acted claims. They point to who Jesus really is.

What is more, the miracles are pictures of what Jesus offers to do in the human heart. His opening of the eyes of a blind beggar whom he encountered, Bartimaeus, is a picture of the new vision he offers to us all. His healing of paralyzed people is a picture of the new power he makes available to those who put their lives in his hand. His turning water into wine at a wedding feast shows how he can transform a life of drudgery and boredom. His feeding of the multitudes shows how he longs to be the bread that satisfies the believer's heart. Jesus wanted to make concrete before the imaginations of his contemporaries – and their successors – the spiritual revolution he was longing to bring into their lives.

Nor must we forget that the preaching of God's kingdom and the marks of that same kingdom marched hand in hand during the ministry of Jesus. He came to proclaim that God's kingly rule had broken out in a fresh way through his ministry, and the miracles underlined that. According to Isaiah, in the future age of salvation the deaf would hear, the blind would see, the lame walk and the mute sing (Isaiah 29:18–19; 35:5–6; 61:1). The miracles proclaimed that this age of salvation had dawned in the person and ministry of Jesus.

Finally, an important purpose of the miracles is to pose a challenge we cannot evade. After all, when you have seen someone raised from the dead in your presence, what are you to make of it? You are driven to make some decision about the one who did it. Is he a quack? Or is he for real? Does he operate by witchcraft? Or by the power of God? None of the miracles constitutes knockdown proof. But they cause you furiously to think. You have to decide about Jesus. Some of those present decided to throw their lot in with him. Others decided they would not only reject him but hound him to his death. Miracles call for a decision.

7. 'JESUS NEVER REALLY WENT TO THE CROSS'

If you have ever have any serious discussion with a Muslim, he or she is sure to come up with the claim that Jesus, whom they recognize and deeply revere as a prophet of God, never died on the cross at all. They have learnt this from the Qur'an.

What does the Qur'an say?

The passage in question comes in sura 4.156f.: 'They said (in boast) "We killed Christ Jesus the Son of Mary, the Messenger of Allah" – but they killed him not nor crucified him, but so it was made to appear to them, and those who differ therein are full of doubts, with no (certain) knowledge, but only conjecture to follow, for of a surety they killed him not. Nay, Allah raised him up unto Himself; and Allah is Exalted in Power, Wise.'

The first thing to notice about this passage is that it does not specifically say that Jesus was not crucified. It is part of a rebuke to Jews for various things, including their opposition to Muhammad, and in passing refers to the crucifixion. It may well be that the Qur'an is simply refuting the boastful claim of the Jews that they had got rid of the Christian Messiah and had repudiated his claim to be an apostle of God by crucifying him. 'They did not kill him, nor did they crucify him' does not necessarily mean that there was no crucifixion, but that it was the Romans, and ultimately God, who were responsible, not the Jews. That is perfectly compatible with the testimony of the New Testament. The experts on Islam quote a somewhat

similar passage in sura 8.17. It refers to the Muslim victory
over the forces of Mecca at the Battle of Badr, and reads,
'It is not ye (Muslims) who slew them ; it was Allah: when
thou, (Muhammad) threwest (a handful of dust) it was not
thy act but Allah's.' The victory which Muhammad and his
forces certainly won, is attributed not to them but to Allah.
The same thing may lie behind the Qur'an's statement about
the cross of Jesus. There are deeper causes for his death
than the Jews.

That may be what the Qur'an is claiming. If so it would
avoid an embarrassing conflict with other verses in the Qur'an
which assert that Jesus did undergo death. A Muslim may well
be reluctant to show you these, and will rely on your not
knowing them.

In the part of the Qur'an which deals with the birth of
Jesus, for example, the baby says to people from his cradle,
'"Peace on me the day I was born, and the day I die, and the
day I shall be raised alive." Such was Jesus the Son of Mary:
it is a statement of truth about which they vainly dispute'(19.33).
Here is a strong truth claim, bizarrely uttered by the baby
Jesus in his cradle, that he will die and rise again! Other references which speak of God gathering Jesus to himself (3.55)
and Jesus being taken (5.117) are somewhat ambiguous and
may possibly mean that Jesus was taken to Allah's side without
experiencing death, but the Arabic word used in both instances,
tawaffa, normally refers to people being called to pay their
dues at death. That would be the natural interpretation of
these two passages. At all events, it is far from clear that the
Qur'an teaches that Jesus was not crucified – though this is
what Muslims are taught to believe. It may simply be the case
that the passage in sura 4 indicates it was the Romans not the
Jews who crucified Jesus and they did so within the permissive
will of God. On any showing sura 19 means what it says – that

the Jesus who was born of Mary would die and be raised again – just as the Christians have always maintained.

However you will often find Muslims arguing that someone else, perhaps Simon of Cyrene, was substituted for Jesus and died on the cross, while Jesus went free. You have to be desperate to argue something like this when there is no evidence for it! However, the Muslims were not the first to make the suggestion. It was actually put forward in the apocryphal *Acts of John*, a sort of Gnostic romance written in the third century AD.

John is represented as having fled at the time of the crucifixion to a cave on the Mount of Olives, and says, 'And my Lord stood in the middle of the cave, and gave light to it and said "John, for the people below, I am being crucified and pierced with lances and reeds and given vinegar and gall to drink. But to you I am speaking, and listen to what I say. I put into your mind to come up to this mountain so that you may hear what a disciple should learn from his teacher and a man of God." And when he had said this he showed me a Cross of Light firmly fixed, and around the Cross a great crowd, which had no single form; and on it was one form and the same likeness. And I saw the Lord himself above the Cross, having no shape but only a kind of voice . . . '

This is very strange stuff, but typical of the Docetic outlook of the Gnostics to which we have already drawn attention. The physical body only seems to be real. But it is unimportant. It is the wisdom and enlightenment imparted to the spirit of the Gnostic that matters. And so here the heavenly Lord speaks words of wisdom to John while the appearance of Jesus (and the Gnostic would not care whether it was Jesus himself or someone substituted for him) was being crucified outside the city walls.

It is probable that Muhammad came across this debased heretical Christianity or something very like it. Maybe that is what he meant in saying, 'so it was made to appear to them', in his statement about the cross. But in any case the idea that Jesus was not crucified would appeal to him. He believed Allah was obliged to protect his prophets. Since Jesus was uniquely born of a virgin, worked miracles, and was the 'Word' of Allah and a 'Spirit' from Allah, all of which is taught in the Qur'an, it was natural to suppose that Allah would look after him. The general teaching of the Qur'an is that Allah gives victory to his prophets and will surely vindicate them. So it was hard for Muhammad, and remains hard for Muslims today, to imagine that God would allow Jesus to undergo such terrible suffering. Islam is a religion of the sword. It has always advanced through conquest or victory in other ways. The concept of vicarious suffering, so central to Christianity, is quite alien to it.

The reliability of sources

We cannot leave this topic without a salutary reminder about the reliability of sources. As far as historical evidence about Jesus is concerned the Qur'an is worthless. It was written in the seventh century AD and the life of Jesus took place six hundred years before that! The death of Jesus on the cross is assured. No scholars other than convinced Muslims deny it. It is one of the agreed points between fundamentalists, conservatives, liberals, revisionists and classical and Jewish scholars. As we saw in chapter four, we read it in the Roman historian Tacitus. We read it in the Jewish historian Josephus, both from the first century. We read it in the four Gospels, also from the first century. It appears in a short creedal statement which Paul the apostle quotes in his letter to the church in Corinth:, 'For what I received I passed on to you as of first importance: that Christ died for our sins according to the Scriptures, that he was buried, that he was raised on the third day according to the Scriptures' (1 Corinthians 15:3–4). This is evidently a pre-Pauline construction familiar both to Paul and the Corinthians, and must date from shortly after the crucifixion itself.

Even more explicit is Philippians 2:5–11, probably the oldest piece in the whole New Testament. It can easily be translated back into Aramaic, the language of Jesus and the first Christians. It tells how Jesus 'being in very nature God' did not hold on to his position but became a man and 'humbled himself and became obedient to death – even death on a cross!' The evidence is unambiguous. If the Qur'an denies it (and as we have seen there is some ambiguity about that) it simply points to the lateness and unreliability of the Qur'an.

There is a wise word of C. S. Lewis that needs to be borne in mind. 'I do not wish to reduce the sceptical element in your minds. I am only suggesting that it need not be reserved exclusively for the New Testament. Try doubting something else!'

8. 'JESUS DID NOT RISE FROM THE DEAD – HIS TOMB HAS BEEN FOUND!'

Is there a life beyond the grave? Or do we go out like a light when we die? Who has not asked questions like these at some time or other in life? All the great religions in the world attempt some answer, however tentative. Christianity certainly does. Indeed the claim that Jesus rose from the dead takes us to the very heart of Christianity. For the Christian faith does not claim that Jesus was a great teacher and a fine man. It maintains that in Jesus God broke into our world. His whole life was a demonstration of what God is like. And when men had crucified him through envy and hatred on the first Good Friday, God raised him from the dead on Easter day, thus vindicating his claims and his teaching, his life and his sacrificial death.

That is and always has been the Christian claim. But many people simply do not believe it. So if you want to examine the credibility of Christianity, it is to the resurrection you must turn. Everything hangs on it. Demonstrate it, and the Christian gospel makes sense. Disprove it, and Christianity falls to the ground. The opponents of Christianity have always recognized this, and there have been concerted attacks on the resurrection from the first century until today. *Jesus Is Dead* is the title Robert Price, my friendly atheist, has given to his recent book. By way of contrast, N. T. Wright, a distinguished New Testament scholar who has written an 817-page book on the subject, *The Resurrection of the Son of God*, concludes, after a magisterial dismissal of alternative theories, 'The proposal that Jesus was bodily raised from the dead possesses unrivalled power to explain the historical data at the heart of early Christianity.'

The 'lost tomb' of Jesus

Wright's book was published a little too early to engage with a television documentary on the Discovery Channel, which caused a great deal of interest and heated controversy in 2007. It was called *The Lost Tomb of Jesus*, and was put out in association with a book, *The Jesus Family Tomb* by Simcha Jacobovici and Charles Pellegrino. The film was directed by James Cameron, and film-maker Simcha Jacobovici. Cameron had earlier presided over the production of the *Titanic*, and this of course gave the project great prestige.

The documentary is all about a large tomb of the Second Temple period (which came to an end in AD 70) at Talpiot, a suburb of Jerusalem. Inside were ten ossuaries, or bone caskets, six of which had rough inscriptions on them, and one of them has since disappeared. The names were fascinating. We find Jesus the son of Jose (= Joseph), Maria (= Mary), Matia (?= Matthew), Mariamne el Mara (?= Mary Magdalene), and Juda son of Jesus.

When allied to the theories of Dan Brown in *The Da Vinci Code*, little imagination is needed to see what a magnificent film this would make. It claims to reveal nothing less than the lost tomb of Jesus of Nazareth. Indeed, it is his family tomb. Mariamne is another name for Mary and Mara may mean she was the master (theologian). Two DNA samples (only!) were taken, one from Mariamne's casket and one from that of Jesus. This demonstrated that they were not related on their mother's side (but they might well have been on the father's side!). Therefore, suggest the filmmakers, they were probably married, or how else would Mary appear in the Jesus family tomb? As for Juda son of Jesus, well, clearly he was their son. Pretty odd to call your son after the man who betrayed you to death, don't you think? They claim that the odds are at least 600 to 1 on this being the family tomb of Jesus.

Unfortunately the whole hypothesis is a tissue of improbabilities and misinformation, and several of the scholars quoted in the film have rejected the use made of their remarks.

The discovery of the Talpiot ossuaries was made in 1980, and I have had the privilege of seeing some of them in the Rockefeller Museum in Jerusalem. So the evidence, touted as new and earth-shattering in the film, is actually more than twenty-five years old. None of the scholars and archaeologists involved in the dig or in subsequent academic discussion during those twenty-five years has ever suggested it was the tomb of Jesus, not until Cameron and Jacobovici in 2007. Amos Kloner, the Israeli professor who led the 1980 excavation and published the official report, says 'Their movie is not serious. They [say they] are "discovering" things, but they haven't discovered anything. They haven't found anything. Everything had already been published.' Again he says, 'There is no basis . . . to identify this as the family of Jesus.'

How can the Israeli professor be so dismissive? There are many reasons. One is the popularity of the names Joseph, Jesus and Mary in the first century. Extensive research has been done on names like this, and it appears that one in four women in Jerusalem in the time of Jesus was called Mary, one in eleven Jesus, one in seven Joseph. Indeed in the years 20 BC to AD 70, out of 80,000 names recorded in Jerusalem, about a thousand were Jesus with Joseph for a father! We already possess another ossuary labelled Jesus son of Joseph. Josephus the Jewish historian records no less than twenty-one men named Jesus.

Of course, other objections spring to mind. Jesus was not known as 'Jesus son of Joseph' – his followers never called him that. There is no evidence, even in the third century

Gnostic gospels which Dan Brown loves so much, that he married anyone, let alone Mary Magdalene. There is no suggestion that he had a son, Juda or anyone else! The Talpiot tomb was extensive – the film-makers omit to tell us that there are thirty-five other unexamined ossuaries in this burial place but the dig had to be closed, back in 1980, because of opposition by Orthodox Jews to its continuance. This makes it less possible than ever that it contained only the family of one person. There are two Marys in the bone caskets and neither of them is called Magdalene. And what would a name like Matia (?= Matthew) be doing in the family tomb of Jesus?

In any case, this was a large middle class burial chamber typical of the fairly well-off in Jerusalem – some eight hundred similar ones have been discovered. Even if a poor family like that of Jesus could have afforded such a tomb, which they could not, would it not have been in Bethlehem where Jesus was born or in Nazareth where he lived his adult life, rather than in Jerusalem where he never lived at all? Indeed the very lettering of his name is controversial. Leading Israeli professor Stephen Pfann told the *National Geographic News*, 'I don't think it says "Yehoshua" (= Jesus). It says "Hanun" or something like that.' And Joe Zias, curator of the Rockefeller Museum, who personally numbered the ossuaries when they were discovered, declared, 'Projects like this [film] make a mockery of the archaeological profession. It makes a great story for a TV film. But it's impossible. It's nonsense.' The historian Paul Maier is even more blunt. 'This is mere naked hype, baseless sensationalism, and nothing less than a media fraud.'

Did Jesus rise from the dead?

All of which brings us back to the fundamental issue. It has never been better expressed than by Professor C. E. M. Joad, a former broadcaster and philosopher who eventually renounced his atheism. He was once asked whom of all past figures in history he would most like to meet, and what he would most like to ask them. He replied that he would most like to meet Jesus Christ, and he would want to ask him the most important question in the world: 'Did you or did you not rise from the dead?' That is the critical question. I propose to approach it from four aspects: I want us to examine our presuppositions, weigh the evidence, reflect on the objections, and consider the consequences. That is what we will do in the remainder of this chapter and in the next.

Examine your presuppositions

We cannot approach a question like this without some prior assumptions and attitudes in our minds. The important thing is to be clear what they are and the extent to which they mask our honest examination of the evidence.

Perhaps the most widespread is apathy, resting on mis-understanding. Many people could not care less whether Jesus did or did not rise from the tomb. They wonder, what does it matter? Actually, it matters a great deal, not just to Christians but to everyone. Apathy is illegitimate because if the resurrection is true it has the most staggering implications for everyone on the planet, and for the destiny of humankind as a whole. As for the misunderstanding, it is that Jesus was just a man like the rest of us, and if he rose from the grave it is rather as if someone who had drowned on Brighton beach was dragged from the sea, given the kiss of life, and resuscitated. Of course, the Christian claim is nothing remotely like this. It is that 'since Christ was raised from the dead, he cannot die again; death no longer has mastery over him' (Romans 6:9). We are not talking about temporary resuscitation, which will in due course be terminated by death proper, but about resurrection from the grip of death to a new and irreversible life. So it matters a great deal that we are clear what we are talking about, and put apathy and misunderstanding aside on this crucial matter.

The second assumption we have already examined in chapter four. The idea of resurrection, we are told, was culled from the mystery religions. And what was originally a reflection of the death and resurrection of vegetation, later applied to mythological deities, came to be attached to Jesus of Nazareth. We have seen that there is no single example of a person's genuine resurrection to be found anywhere in ancient history before that attributed to Jesus. To claim otherwise is baseless prejudice.

A third assumption is very widespread. The resurrection, we feel, is scientifically impossible. 'When I die, I rot,' wrote Bertrand Russell, the celebrated philosopher. And recently James Tabor in his book *The Jesus Dynasty* (2006) has put it very clearly: 'Dead bodies don't rise – not if one is clinically dead – as surely Jesus was.' In other words, the resurrection must be ruled out of court. It is impossible.

Well, such dogmatism is not the normal way in which reputable scientists examine a problem. True, there is impatience with miracle in many scientific circles, but it is matched by an increasing recognition of the limitations of our knowledge and the mystery of the universe.

There are just two points that deserve to be borne in mind with regard to science and the resurrection.

The first concerns scientific method, which is unashamedly inductive. That is to say, it does not begin with a theory and then seek facts to back it up, but begins with the phenomena that present themselves and then seeks to arrive at a generalization which could account for them. It does not begin by ruling out of order facts that are inconvenient. Instead it examines them. Many of the advances in scientific enquiry have taken place when scientists have wrestled with the one awkward fact which did not fit into the prevailing theory. In principle there is no scientific reason why Jesus should not have risen from the grave if he was indeed God's Son. The question is, did he?

There is a second point that needs to be made to James Tabor and those who think like him. We are not claiming that there is a certain class of people that defy death and get up out of their coffins. The first-century writers were not so naïve as to claim that. What they maintained is that Jesus was no ordinary man. They came to believe that in this very exceptional person, one who was more than a man, the forces of death met their match. We saw in chapter one some of the reasons that led them to this assessment of Jesus, and shall see more in the next chapter. How then could they – or, for that matter we ourselves – be sure that he could not overcome death? He lived an unsullied life, perfect at every point. How could they – or we – be sure that the only life which had given no foothold to sin could not master death? We have no other example of the 'sinless' category to compare him with. Jesus made the whole of his credibility rest on the assertion that he would 'do a Jonah' on his contemporaries; and just as the ancient prophet Jonah came back from his three day 'death' inside the great fish, so Jesus himself would come back from the jaws of death (Matthew 12:39–41).

So it is appropriate to lay aside the dogmatic prejudice which asserts, 'It could never happen', and examine whether, according to the evidence available to us, it *did* happen in this one solitary case of Jesus. If he was perfect in his humanity, if he was more than a man, we cannot arbitrarily rule it out of court.

We should not allow prejudice to keep us from examining the evidence of the New Testament. It is no good claiming that modern people will not credit the resurrection, or that its historicity is irrelevant once its symbolic force is granted. In sheer integrity, we must lay aside presuppositions of this nature and look at the evidence.

9. 'JESUS DID NOT RISE FROM THE DEAD – THERE'S NO EVIDENCE'

John Lennon, in an interview, admitted that Santa Claus was more real to him than Jesus. He saw no evidence for Christ's resurrection, believing that the 'stuff about magic and miracles' was written much later. He was disenchanted with the claims of Christians about miracles and Jesus rising from the dead. He said, 'This is the Christ-bit, you know, "Give yourself to Christ." A: He's dead. B: Prove it to me.'

Weigh the evidence

John Lennon, like many others, quite reasonably wanted some proofs of the Christian claims. It will be a surprise to many that there is any evidence for the resurrection of Jesus from the dead. They think that Christians are whistling in the wind to keep their spirits up. The truth of the matter is that the evidence is both extensive and challenging. We shall only have space to examine a fraction of it.

The evidence of the crucifixion

The first thing to be clear about is that Jesus was definitely dead. Crucifixion was ruthlessly efficient. There is only one example of any crucified person surviving. It happened when the Jewish ex-general Josephus saw three friends of his being nailed to a cross. He immediately begged the Roman commander Titus, soon to become emperor, for the life of his friends. Titus acceded: the men were immediately taken down from the cross, and given the best medical care available. Nevertheless two of them expired from their wounds.

Jesus died in an unusually quick time, six hours or so. The executioners came to examine him before a friend of his, Joseph of Arimathea, was allowed to take the body down for burial. These soldiers were experienced at their grisly task: crucifixions were common in Palestine. They knew a dead man when they saw one – and their commanding officer had heard the condemned man's death-cry himself, and certified Jesus as dead to the provincial governor, Pontius Pilate (Mark 15:39, 44). Had he got this important matter wrong, the officer's life might have been forfeit. But just to make doubly sure, the squad pierced his heart through with a spear. And then a very remarkable thing happened.

We are told on eyewitness authority that 'blood and water' came out of the pierced side of Jesus (John 19:34f.). The eyewitness clearly attached great importance to this. Had Jesus been alive when the spear pierced his side, strong spurts of bright arterial blood would have emerged with every heart-beat. Instead, the observer noticed a semi-solid dark red clot seeping out, distinct and separate from the accompanying watery serum. This is evidence of massive clotting of the blood in the main arteries, and is exceptionally strong medical proof of death. It is all the more impressive because the gospel writer could not possibly have realized its significance to a pathologist. The 'blood and water' from the spear-thrust is proof positive that Jesus was already dead, and as a result all the hypotheses that rest on his supposed resuscitation in the cool of the tomb can be ruled out of court.

The evidence of the empty tomb
After the death of Jesus was certified Pilate, we read, ceded the body to Joseph of Arimathea (Mark 15:45). The word

used for 'body' is significant: it is not *soma*, the normal word for body, but *ptoma*, which is always used of a dead body. The corpse would have been placed on a stone ledge, wound in strips of cloth, and covered with spices. John's Gospel tells us that some seventy-five pounds were used, and that is likely enough. Joseph was a rich senator, and no doubt wanted to make up for the cowardliness of his long allegiance to Jesus by giving him a splendid funeral. The amount, though great, has parallels. Rabbi Gamaliel, a contemporary of Jesus, was buried with eighty pounds of spices when he died.

But details like this make nonsense of the theory, alluded to above, that Jesus was not really dead, and that after reviving in the cool of the tomb he crept out and persuaded his gullible disciples that he was risen from the dead. That rationalistic refuge from the powerful evidence for the resurrection has a long ancestry. It was produced by Schleiermacher in 1799, and was revived a few decades ago by Hugh Schonfield in *The Passover Plot* (1965). But it has nothing to commend it. It ignores the finality of Roman crucifixions, the examination by experienced executioners, the blood and water, the governor's handing over of the corpse, the constricting grave-clothes, the crushing weight of spices, the lack of human help, and the sealed tomb. What is more, it is psychologically impossible. How could someone who crept practically dead out of the tomb, needing bandaging, recovery time and every care, have given the impression to anyone that he was Lord of life and conqueror over the grave?

The tomb was empty

Jesus was dead and buried. And every scrap of evidence from the period is unanimous that on the third day the tomb was found to be empty. Matthew, Mark, Luke, John, Peter, the virgin Mary, and Mary Magdalene are all clear about it. So, by inference, is the apostle Paul.

At this point it may be relevant to allude to a piece of pagan evidence which seems to support the story of the resurrection. It is called the Nazareth inscription, after the town where it was found, which was of course the home town of Jesus. It is an imperial edict, belonging either to the reign of Tiberius (AD 14–37) or Claudius (AD 41–54). And it is an invective, backed with heavy sanctions, against meddling around with tombs! It looks very much as if the news of the empty tomb had got back to Rome in a garbled form. Pilate would have had to report: and he would obviously have said that the tomb had been rifled. This edict, it would appear, is the imperial reaction. It speaks of extracting the buried, transferring them to other places, or displacing the seal on the tomb. And it demands capital punishment for the convicted offender – an extremely unusual and serious penalty, which indicates the intense anxiety of an emperor, determined to shut the door after the horse had bolted!

Whatever we make of the Nazareth inscription, there can be no doubt that the tomb of Jesus was in fact empty on the first Easter day. The only alternative explanation will not stand investigation for a minute. A scholar called Kirsopp Lake proposed that, in their overwrought state, the women visited the wrong tomb in the dim light of the Easter dawn, and were directed to the right one by a young man who happened to be around early. 'You are looking for Jesus the Nazarene, who was crucified. . . . He is not here. See the place where they laid him' (Mark 16:6). The women were, of course, terrified and ran away. Later they made the young man out to be an angel and his words to be an announcement of the resurrection.

Ingenious, but it will not do. For one thing it leaves out the crucial words the young man is reported to have said: '*He has risen*. He is not here.' For another, it is highly unconvincing to suppose that the three women who had so lovingly and courageously attended to the last rites of Jesus on the Friday evening should, a mere thirty-six hours later, all have been mistaken about the location of the grave that they themselves had helped to get ready! Indeed, Mark almost seems to go out of his way to anticipate this objection by ending his account of Friday evening in this way: 'Mary Magdalene and Mary the mother of Joses took a good long look [that is the meaning of *etheoroun*] at where he was laid' (Mark 15:47, my translation). But the complete refutation of the theory is easy.

If the right tomb was known, why on earth was the right body not produced as soon as the resurrection began to be proclaimed? That would have scotched the movement at the start. But that is what nobody could do. The body was not to be found. But the grave-clothes were! They lay as they had when wrapped around his body, but collapsed like a chrysalis case when the butterfly has emerged. It was this sight that convinced Peter and John that Jesus had risen from the dead (John 20:3–9). For what grave-robber would strip the corpse and arrange so elaborate a charade?

The evidence of the appearances of Jesus

For a period of six weeks after the resurrection Jesus appeared to his disciples to convince them that he was indeed alive, and that the most remarkable miracle since the creation of the world had taken place. Sometimes he appeared to the whole group of eleven disciples, gathered in the upper room they had come to treat as home. Sometimes it was to a couple of disciples walking in the country. Once we find him making breakfast for a group of them who had been out on a night of fruitless fishing. But the most remarkable thing in this whole remarkable business is that the first witnesses of the risen Jesus were women (Matthew 28:1, 9 and John 20:11ff.). Remember that in antiquity, in both Jewish and secular society, the testimony of a woman counted for nothing! If anybody had been making up these stories we can be certain that they would not have made the first witnesses women! The primacy given to women in meeting the risen Christ is a strong indication of authenticity.

The most important list of these appearances, however, comes in 1 Corinthians 15. It is a passage worth quoting in full. 'For what I received', writes Paul, 'I passed on to you as of first importance: that Christ died for our sins according to the Scriptures, that he was buried, that he was raised on the third day according to the Scriptures, and that he appeared to Peter, and then to the Twelve. After that, he appeared to more than five hundred of the brothers at the same time, most of whom are still living, though some have fallen asleep. Then he appeared to James, then to all the apostles, and last of all he appeared to me also, as to one abnormally born' (verses 3–8).

That is a fascinating list, for all sorts of reasons. First, it was written by a man who had been the arch enemy of Christians before his conversion. Second, the repeated 'that' is a device in Greek to show that he is quoting. And the material he is citing is very old. So old that he tells us it was traditional before he became a Christian – for that is what 'passed on' and 'received' mean: they are technical terms for the receiving and transmitting of authorized tradition. Paul is quoting material going back to the very earliest days of the church. So it is impossible to exaggerate the importance of this list. It is possibly the oldest thing in the New Testament.

Notice that it does not attempt to prove the resurrection: you do not prove historical events – you amass convincing eyewitness testimony to them. That is what Paul does here. And what are these witnesses claiming? Not that they saw Jesus rise from the dead. Nobody in the New Testament (in contrast to the later apocryphal gospels) claims that – but something at once more sober and more far-reaching. They bear witness to the fact that Jesus not only rose but is alive. This comes out clearly from the tenses used in this passage. 'Died', 'was buried', and 'appeared' are all in the aorist tense – normal for past action. But the verb translated, 'he was raised', abruptly breaks the sequence of tenses and sticks out like a sore thumb. For it is in the perfect tense. And the perfect is used of a past event when the effects remain until the present. So in that single word *egegertai* we see two crucial points. Not only did he rise on the third day, as a fact of history: *he is still alive*, and that is something which believers can experience for themselves.

Such was the earliest Christian assertion about the resurrection: a matter of history and a matter of experience. And it really is astonishingly early. Paul writes to the Corinthians in AD 53. He is not informing them of the resurrection for the first time, but reminding them of the emphasis he had placed on it when he preached the gospel to them, two years earlier. And he reminds them that he had passed on to them what he had himself received as creedal tradition. Paul himself must have been converted in AD 33 or 34 in order to fit the evidence of Galatians 2:1 and the Jerusalem Council of Acts 15, held in AD 49. In other words the tradition of the Lordship of Jesus, his death and resurrection, can be traced back to the year or two after the resurrection, and this is now recognized even by scholars of the Jesus Seminar. There is no evidence in the whole of ancient history stronger than this.

Paul's words here certainly constitute a staggering claim. What witnesses support it? First, 'he appeared to Peter'. The

Peter who denied he ever knew Jesus. We do not know what took place in this very intimate interview, which is referred to with the same tantalizing reserve in Luke 24:34. But it was clearly a time of forgiveness and re-commissioning, and Peter became the fearless spokesman of the earliest church. It was the resurrection that made all the difference.

Second, Jesus appeared to 'the Twelve' (eleven, actually, since Judas had committed suicide). How is it that this pathetic group which forsook Jesus at his hour of need, became the bold apostles whom we meet in the Acts? They were indomitable. They faced scorn, opposition, persecution, and death in three continents as they preached the gospel of Jesus. What was it that changed them? It was the resurrection.

'All the apostles' are mentioned, and this must include Thomas. He was very sceptical about the resurrection – and who can blame him? But when Jesus appeared to him and invited him to inspect his wounds in hands and side, Thomas fell to the ground and made the strongest profession of faith of all the disciples, 'My Lord and my God' (John 20:26ff.).

'The five hundred' who all saw Jesus at the same time are interesting. They were probably from Galilee where Jesus had done most of his ministry. Paul realizes that in the twenty-year interval between the event and his writing to the Corinthians some of them will have died, but the majority of them were still alive, and could testify to having met the risen Jesus. We know no more about them, but they are the precursors of countless millions who have borne witness to the resurrection ever since.

Two names are very significant in this list. James was the Lord's brother, and did not believe in him during Jesus' earthly ministry (John 7:5). But before long we find him leading the early church in Jerusalem (Acts 15:13). What changed him from a sceptic to a major Christian leader? It was the resurrection. 'He appeared to James.' The other name, equally amazing, is that of Paul himself. He was the most passionate persecutor of the first Christians (Acts 9:1ff.) and yet he was so soundly converted by meeting the risen Christ that he became Christianity's most famous and effective evangelist. What changed him? It was the resurrection.

N. T. Wright, in *The Resurrection of the Son of God*, argues persuasively that neither the empty tomb by itself nor the resurrection appearances by themselves would validate the resurrection, but together they do. They furnish a sufficient and necessary explanation of the faith of the Christian church. The point is well made by the secular historian J. M. Roberts in his *History of Europe*:

> Whatever may be thought of the Gospel records, it cannot plausibly be maintained that they were written by men who did not believe these things, nor that they did not write down what they were told by men and women who believed they had seen some of them with their own eyes. Clearly, too, Jesus' life was not so successful in a worldly sense that his teaching was likely to survive because of the impact of his ethical message alone. He had, it is true, especially attracted many of the poor and outcast, as well as Jews who felt that their traditions or the forms of behavior into which they had hardened were no longer satisfactory. But these successes would have died with him had his disciples not believed that he had conquered death itself and that those who were saved by being baptized as his followers would also overcome death and live for ever after God's judgment. Before a century had passed, this message was being preached throughout the whole civilized world united and sheltered by the Roman empire.

The evidence of the launch of the church

The birthday of the church follows naturally on what we have seen above – it can be traced back to the first Easter. Shortly after the crucifixion of Jesus an entirely new religious movement began which spread like wildfire. This is undeniable. Its members made it plain that they were the community of the resurrection. They proclaimed the death, resurrection and Lordship of Jesus.

Associated with the rise of the church are several subordinate but significant things. The Christians had two sacraments. One was baptism, the sacrament of Christian initiation. The other was the Eucharist, the sacrament of Christian growth. Both were rooted in the resurrection. In baptism the candidate symbolically died to sin and rose to new life with the risen Christ. In the Eucharist they believed the risen Lord was in their midst as they took the tokens of his death for them, the broken bread and the outpoured wine. That is why they celebrated it with *agalliasis*, exultation (Acts 2:46). Both sacraments would have been a complete travesty had the resurrection not been a core conviction of the first Christians.

In addition to the sacraments, there was the preaching of the good news of salvation. The heart of this was that the long-awaited Messiah had come, had been killed, and was risen from the grave and designated Lord of the universe. That was another remarkable aspect of the church's life, which would be impossible to explain, had the resurrection not been at the forefront of their belief. On top of all this, they succeeded in changing the day of rest from its time-honoured Saturday to Sunday, the day of resurrection. That was a phenomenal achievement. It indicated that they saw the resurrection as even more significant than the creation of the world, commemorated in Judaism by the sabbath. It is not easy to change the day of rest. Try moving it to

Monday! Something very significant had happened – the resurrection.

Taken together, the empty tomb, the resurrection appearances and the rise of the church furnish very powerful evidence for the resurrection of Jesus from the grave. But there is one further element which is perhaps more important than any of them. It is the changed lives of believers. We have noted it in the transformation of the first disciples. It has continued throughout history. Millions upon millions have been able to say, 'I know Jesus is alive. I am in daily touch with him.' And their lives back up their claim. They experience something of his love, his power, his answers to their prayers and his presence, which assure them beyond contradiction that Jesus Christ is risen from the dead.

As I write I have before me the testimony of a twenty-seven-year-old barrister who called himself a free thinker until his life was turned upside down by an encounter with Christ. There is another, a young woman who was immersed in Feng Shui and crystals which she thought could predict the future – until she discovered the living Christ, at an Alpha course. This is happening to some 70,000 people a day, so the statisticians say. It is not proof. But it is mighty powerful evidence!

Reflect on the objections

Needless to say, the resurrection is so staggering that people will go to great lengths to deny it. We have already examined a couple of the objections commonly raised. Here are some others.

'The apostle Paul, our earliest witness, knew nothing of the empty tomb'

It is undoubtedly true that Paul is much more interested in

the risen Jesus than he is in the emptiness of the tomb. But there are three pieces of evidence in our earliest document, 1 Corinthians 15, which show that Paul was well aware that the tomb of Jesus was empty. This was written just twenty years after the event.

In the first place, he quotes as 'of first importance' the very early piece of tradition passed on to him when he was converted to Christianity in the mid thirties, shortly after the resurrection itself. He maintains that Jesus was raised *on the third day*. What does this extremely early tradition imply? It must mean here, as in Peter's assertion in Acts (for example, 10:40), that on the third day the tomb of Jesus was found to be empty, and Jesus was encountered, alive. The mention of that third day is decisive. It must show that Paul knew about the empty tomb.

Secondly, when Jews spoke about resurrection, they meant only one thing. They did not mean the survival of the soul, for the Hebrews regarded human personality as a unity. They meant bodily resurrection at the culmination of all history, and not before. They would not know what to make of the 'spiritual survival' which some modern writers want to attribute to Paul's understanding of the resurrection. To a Jew, if Jesus' bones were still in a Palestinian tomb, there could be no argument about it. He could not, in that case, be described as 'risen'.

Throughout 1 Corinthians 15 Paul asserts the reality of the resurrection in the most robust terms. He was a Jew, and could not exclude the physical from his understanding of resurrection. Indeed the Pharisees used to argue whether you would be raised with the wart on your nose that you had in this life! You can search the Rabbinic writings in vain to find any mention of a purely 'spiritual' resurrection. Furthermore, when you recall that all the earliest believers in the risen Christ were Jews, when you remember that 'a large number of the priests became obedient to the faith' (Acts 6:7), then it is simply naïve – or escapism – to claim that a 'spiritual' resurrection will cover the facts. When Paul said 'risen' he meant 'physically risen'. 'If Christ has not been raised, your faith is futile; you are still in your sins . . . If only for this life we have hope in Christ, we are to be pitied more than all men' (1 Corinthians 15:17, 19).

The third piece of evidence that Paul took the empty tomb for granted, and simply assumed it without argument when he says 'died . . . was buried . . . was raised' is this. He goes to some lengths to explain, in the second part of this long chapter, that our destiny is to be made like Christ. We shall have a resurrection body, as Jesus had. 'Just as we have borne the likeness of the earthly man, so shall we bear the likeness of the man from heaven. . . . It is sown a natural body, it is raised a spiritual body. If there is a natural body, there is also a spiritual body' (1 Corinthans 15:49, 44). Just as the physical body of Jesus was transformed at the resurrection, so it will be with the Christian, who will exchange this body subject to decay for a body that is imperishable. This sort of analogy would be utterly impossible if Paul did not think Jesus' body had been physically raised.

There can be no doubt, then, that the apostle Paul knew the tradition of the empty tomb and accepted it without bothering to discuss it. After all, he mentions that Jesus was buried. What would be the point of that if not to indicate that on the third day the tomb was unoccupied, because God had raised Jesus to a new life, beyond the reach of death?

'The resurrection appearances were hallucinations'
This is an important challenge, because if it could be demonstrated that the resurrection appearances were hallucinations

this would bring about the collapse not of a single doctrine only but the whole structure of Christianity. Let us see if it bears critical scrutiny.

Normally only certain personality types are subject to hallucinations. Someone like Mary Magdalene might fill the bill, but not people of such diverse temperaments as Peter, Paul, Thomas and James. Hallucinations are normally individual things. It is noticeable how weak is the evidence for group hallucinations. But in the case of Jesus the same 'hallucination' is observed by fishermen, tax collectors, rabbis, close relations, a determined foe and five hundred people at once.

Hallucinations generally come to people who have been hankering after something for a long time. The wish becomes father to the thought. But here we find no wish fulfilment. As we have seen, the disciples were not expecting anything of the kind, and they proved most reluctant to accept even the evidence of their own eyes.

Hallucinations tend to recur over long periods. Someone who suffers from obsessional appearances continues to suffer from them. But here they ceased as dramatically as they began. It all took place within six weeks.

Hallucinations are generally restricted to a particular person, a particular time and a particular place. In this case, the diversity could not have been more marked. The appearances took place at early morning, at noon, in the afternoon and at night. Seashore, roadside, upper room, garden – the locality made no difference. And those who experienced these 'seeings' were a very varied crowd.

The appearances did not become increasingly bizarre, as is often the case with repeated visions. Rather, they remained very restrained, indeed uniform in character. The contrast with the Gnostic gospels is dramatic in this respect. Moreover, far from mounting in frequency and pitch, as hallucinations often do, these meetings ceased entirely after forty days, never to return. They had served their purpose.

Hallucinations, of course, do not have the physical element which we have seen to be such a marked strand in the resurrection stories. They are not in any sense objective. Nor do they tend to produce in those who have them a remarkable change of character from dishonesty to truthfulness, from fear to confidence, from sorrow to joy – in short, hallucinations are incapable of accounting for the rise, the maintenance and the worldwide spread of the Christian community, and scarcely any theologians nowadays claim that they are. The Easter faith did not manufacture the facts. On the contrary, the Easter event gave rise to this astonishing and world-changing faith.

'The resurrection is not a historical event'
Another of the objections sometimes brought against the resurrection of Jesus is that it is speculative and probably unhistorical. There are a good many sophisticated people, not least theologians, who maintain that we can know nothing about what happened at Easter. The most celebrated was Rudolf Bultmann, the German New Testament, scholar who wrote: 'Can the resurrection narratives and every other mention of the resurrection be understood simply as an attempt to convey the meaning of the cross? . . . Yes indeed . . . ' Again, 'the resurrection itself is not an event in past history. All that historical criticism can establish is the fact that the first disciples came to believe in the resurrection.' He even argues that 'the historical problem is scarcely relevant to Christian belief in the resurrection'.

Bultmann rightly saw that the cross and resurrection belong together in the Christian proclamation. He rightly saw that the empty tomb is far less important than the presence of the risen Christ in the gospel message and in the believer. But then he abandons faith in the physical resurrection of Jesus, locates his Christian confidence in the preached message, and construes the Easter faith as meaning that the cross, which he regards as the climax of the Jesus story, has saving significance. Bultmann was a complicated character. Many influences affected him – the scepticism of Lessing and Wrede, the existentialism of Heidegger, as well as Luther's emphasis on the word of God. However there are three crucial questions we must ask of his position.

First, granted the importance of the Easter faith, what Easter *event* gave rise to it? Something assuredly did, and it cannot be irrelevant to ask whether or not that faith is well grounded.

Second, if Jesus did not rise from the dead, what is the point of saying that he is the living Lord to be met in the Christian preaching? Bultmann wants us to respond to the preaching, not to argue with it. Fair enough, but only if the proclamation is true!

Third, if history is inimical to Christianity, then Christianity is false and it is much more honest to abandon it. Some of Bultmann's followers on the continent have taken precisely that step and become atheists. However, as we have seen, the fact of the matter is that that there is very strong, very varied and very widespread evidence for the historicity of the Easter event, and none of the attempts to dissolve it into mythology have proved convincing. Christianity is not the mystery religion that happened to succeed. It is all about the God who raised Jesus from the dead.

Consider the consequences

When the apostle Paul discusses the resurrection at length in 1 Corinthians 15 he shows a ruthless integrity in drawing the inferences. If Jesus did not rise from the dead, then Paul's preaching has been a waste of time, the faith of believers is futile, and they remain unforgiven. Moreover Christians misrepresent God, dead Christians are finished, and live Christians are deluded. On the other hand, if Christ did rise from the grave, then he is alive and can be met. He has cleared our accusing past at the cross, he has broken the fear of death, he can change human nature, and his resurrection is the pledge of our own. In other words, it is very hard to exaggerate the importance of the resurrection of Jesus.

Modern people, however, remain unimpressed. When it comes to religion, they are not asking, 'Did Jesus rise from the dead?' but much broader questions like 'Is there a God?', 'Aren't all religions much the same?' and 'What happens after death?' They are quite unaware that the resurrection of Jesus gives us the clue to precisely these questions.

The most compelling argument for *the existence of God*, and the sort of God described in scripture, is Jesus Christ. Jesus never argued for God's existence. He took it for granted. He called God his *Abba*, his dear heavenly father. He claimed that he had been entrusted with God's power to forgive sins, with the privilege of accepting worship as his due, and with the role of final Judge of humankind – utterly mind-boggling prerogatives. But if the resurrection happened, it validates those claims. It shows that, as the apostle Paul put it, Jesus was 'declared with power to be the Son of God, by his resurrection from the dead' (Romans 1:4). It is the clinching evidence for those claims he made during his earthly life.

Jesus has shown us that God is real. He has shown us what God is like. He has shown that God is love. He has shown that God is holy. He has shown that God forgives – at infinite personal cost. He has shown us, by the resurrection, that evil and suffering will not have the last word in God's universe. In the risen Christ we have the answer to our doubts about God.

The resurrection speaks equally powerfully to our questions about *the variety of religions in the world*. My suggestion would be that you do not waste a lot of time and effort examining every religion from Hinduism to animism (a recent TV series was called 'Around the World in 80 Faiths'!). Instead, have a good long look at the resurrection of Jesus Christ. If he rose from the dead, you need look no further. You will find lots to admire and to learn from in other faiths (as well as degradation and cruelty at times): God has not left himself without witness throughout his world. But you will not, I think, find in them anything that you know to be good and true which cannot be found, explicitly or implicitly, in the religion of Jesus. And nowhere else will you hear of a God who cares enough for you to die for you, to rise from the grave as a pledge of the future he offers you, and to be willing to actually come and share your life with you. If Jesus really did rise from the dead, then he is indeed the Way to God, the Truth about God, and the Life of God (John 14:6). In that case, the exclusiveness of the Christian claim makes sense.

It is not that Christians are narrow-minded and uncharitable about other faiths. But if Jesus is indeed, as the resurrection asserts, God who has come to our rescue, then to reject him is the ultimate folly. That is why Jesus is not, and never can be, just one among the religious leaders of the world. How many of the others have vindicated their claims by rising from the dead?

What happens after death? I guess every human being who has ever lived has asked that question. The answers to it are all vague and tentative – except one. The resurrection of Jesus gives a very clear and decisive answer to this question. He has, said C. S. Lewis, in his book *Miracles*, 'forced open a door that had been locked since the death of the first man. He has met, fought, and beaten the King of Death. Everything is different because He has done so. This is the beginning of the New Creation. A new chapter in cosmic history has opened.'

In the Middle Ages there was much speculation in the West as to whether there could be a sea route to India around the southern tip of Africa. Nobody knew for sure, though many hoped against hope that there was. All attempts at rounding the Cape had failed. So much so that this treacherous headland was called the Cape of Storms, as it had been the scene of so many wrecks. However, one courageous mariner determined to try again. Vasco da Gama succeeded in rounding the Cape and reached the East – where a monument to him exists to this very day. Ever since he sailed back to Lisbon in triumph, it has been impossible to doubt that there is a way to the Orient round the bottom of Africa. The very name of that perilous cape was changed to the Cape of Good Hope!

The enigma of life after death is rather like that. Until the time when Jesus died and rose again, death was like that Cape of Storms, littered with wrecks. Until his successful rounding of that cape and return, people had nothing but speculation to go on about any afterlife. Now we know. His resurrection has turned death into the Cape of Good Hope. His resurrection has opened up to us the way to a new and rich land which he has shown exists. And because he has safely circumnavigated that dangerous cape he is well equipped to act as pilot to others. Christian optimism about the future is not facile, but founded on the solid basis of the resurrection of Jesus Christ from the dead. And this same Jesus promised his followers that he would go and prepare a place for them so that where he is, they might be also (John 14:2–3).

The resurrection shows us clearly that there is a God, that Jesus is the way to God, and that death for the Christian leads into the nearer presence of God. No wonder Easter is the prime Christian festival!

10. 'NOBODY THOUGHT JESUS DIVINE UNTIL THE FOURTH CENTURY'

The claim

Every now and again a book emerges which claims that the idea of Jesus' divinity is late and not to be trusted. Back in the 1970s a group of radical scholars produced *The Myth of God Incarnate*, which was a symposium of essays writing off the divinity of Jesus as mythical or poetic but certainly not corresponding to reality. He was a human being like anyone else.

Michael Goulder, one of the contributors to that volume, astonishingly attributes belief in the deity of Christ to the supposed influence of Simon Magus on the church, as well as to the psychological impact of Peter's experience of the (mythical!) resurrection and the subsequent 'power of hysteria within a small community'.

Professor John Hick in the same volume finds it 'natural and intelligible that Jesus . . . should come to be hailed as son of God, and that later this poetry should have hardened into prose, and escalated from a metaphorical son of God to a metaphysical God the Son'.

The book was carelessly composed, embracing various contradictions between the authors and a number of different (and unreconciled) meanings of 'myth'. A corrective was published by a group of scholars who had no difficulty in showing the shortcomings and poor scholarship of this book. It was called *The Truth of God Incarnate*. And there the matter rested – for a while.

Dan Brown's *The Da Vinci Code* was a phenomenal success when it appeared, in dramatic contrast to his earlier books.

Everyone was reading it. And not surprising, for it is a superb thriller. But a great number of readers were fascinated by its sub-plot, which contains a mixture of suspense, sensuality, spiritual search, superstition and revised paganism, while it sets out to undermine the credibility of the New Testament, the divinity of Jesus, and the witness of the church, particularly the Roman Catholic Church. We have had occasion to look at it in a previous chapter.

Brown asserts that Jesus was not divine, and was never thought to be until the Council of Nicea in AD 325, when the matter was put to the vote and just scraped through. It was there, according to Teabing (a royal historian in the story), 'that many aspects of Christianity were debated and voted upon' including 'the divinity of Jesus'. Sophie Neveu, the beautiful cryptologist to whom Teabing expounds this theory, is shocked. '"I don't follow. His divinity?" "My dear", said Teabing, "until *that* moment in history Jesus was viewed by His followers as a mortal prophet . . . a great and powerful man, but a *man* nevertheless. A mortal." "Not the Son of God?" "Right," Teabing said. "Jesus' establishment as 'the Son of God' was officially proposed and voted on by the Council of Nicea." "Hold on. You're saying Jesus' divinity was the result of a *vote*?" "A relatively close vote at that,"' Teabing replies.

The fictional historian goes on to argue that all this was a clever move on the part of the first Christian emperor, Constantine, who chose to strengthen his shaky power base by making the populous movement of Christianity the official religion of the Empire, and upgrading the status of Jesus from mere mortal to that of Son of God. '"To rewrite the history books, Constantine knew he would need a bold stroke. From this sprang the most profound moment in Christian history . . . Constantine commissioned and financed a new Bible, which omitted those gospels which spoke of Christ's *human* traits and embellished those gospels that made Him godlike. The earlier gospels [and by these he means the Gnostic gospels] were outlawed, gathered up, and burned."'

All this is a far cry from the sophisticated argumentation of *The Myth of God Incarnate*, and much more fun. After all, this is a novel and it makes use of liberal doses of imaginative writing. But it sounds very plausible, and for those who do not know much about the background, it looks convincing. Lots of people are taken in by it. So it is worth noting the main points which Brown is making. They are pretty radical. First, the whole collection of books we have in our New Testament were selected by Constantine in the fourth century to serve his purposes. Second, the Gnostic gospels are earlier than our Gospels and superior to them. Third, Jesus was never thought of as divine until those fourth century days when Constantine hit on the brilliant idea of divinizing him.

Let's examine these in turn, the first two briefly, and the third at greater depth, since the deity of Jesus is so central to the message of the Christian gospel, and if it is a fourth-century invention, then Christianity can safely be cast aside.

Brown's first point can be speedily dismissed. After he built his new capital city, Constantinople, the emperor, wrote to Bishop Eusebius, the most distinguished historian and Bible scholar of his day, and asked him to send fifty copies of the Christian scriptures in Greek for the churches of that city. What Eusebius sent was not only identical with our present Bible, but represented the solid witness of the previous one hundred and fifty years as to what books should be included. Needless to say, Constantine did not select a single one of them!

Secondly, Brown wants us to believe that the Gnostic gospels are earlier than the ones we have in our Bible, but that they were 'outlawed, gathered up, and burned'. He would very much like this to be true because, as we saw, much of the sub-plot in his novel is based on elements in the *Gospel of Philip* and the *Gospel of Mary*. Unfortunately for him however, these books emerged some time late in the third century AD, well after our four Gospels, which were all completed by the last quarter of the first century. What is more, they never appear in any list of New Testament books. So Brown's theory that they were earlier than our Gospels and got 'gathered up and burned' by the wicked Constantine and his henchmen is totally without foundation. These so-called gospels, written in the third century, were not really gospels at all. They have no interest in the birth, life, and teaching of the historical Jesus. Instead they are a hotbed of the secret lore and fantastic speculations so beloved by the Gnostics.

As we have seen, the Gnostics believed the world was created by an evil god, inferior to the supreme God from whom their own spirits sprang. This evil God was the God of the Old Testament. The material world which he had made was evil, and the aim of true religion was for their spirits to escape from this material world and from our physical bodies. These Gnostics claimed that they were chips off the old block of the supreme God, to whom they would return at death. They had been awakened to this fact by a special 'imparting' of hidden wisdom and knowledge, which has its residue in the gospels and other documents they came to write, a number of which have come to light in the sands of Egypt. Their beliefs, a mixture of pagan and Christian, were selfish, elitist, anti-feminist, and destructive of true Christianity. The Christian church overcame them in due course, but not without a massive struggle. It is to the documents of these people that Dan Brown loves to turn, along with a whole host of other recent writers who make up fantastic scenarios, particularly involving Mary Magdalene. But the plain fact is that the church never accepted these strange writings, but attacked them vociferously. Moreover, these books emerged long after our New Testament was written and revered as authoritative.

Did the first Christians see Jesus as divine?

The most serious of the claims made both by people like Dan Brown and the scholars who compiled *The Myth of God Incarnate* is that Jesus was not considered divine in the early days of Christianity. So let us examine the assertions of the New Testament writers themselves and see whether they believed in the divinity of Jesus, and whether they intended their words to be taken as poetry or prose, myth or sober fact.

The claim of Paul

Let us begin with a couple of references in the letters of the apostle Paul. He was writing in the fifties of the first century, a mere twenty-five years or so after the death of Jesus. In Colossians 1:15–23, Paul is rebutting the syncretizing tendencies at the city of Colossae, with its many fancied mediators between God and humanity. He asserts that the 'image' of the God we cannot see is located in 'the Son he loves' alone. He is the 'firstborn over all creation' ('firstborn', a fascinating word with a complex history, had long ceased to be used exclusively in its literal sense, and came to denote priority in rank as well as in time). Paul leaves us in no doubt what he means by the word, for 'by him were all things created'.

Not only does he see Christ as the source of creation; but he is the goal of the whole universe, since 'all things were created . . . for him'. As if that were not enough, Paul has so clear a grasp of the cosmic significance of Jesus the Messiah, that he adds, 'in him all things hold together'. Christ is the principle of coherence in the universe. Moreover, he is the 'firstborn from among the dead', the pledge of the Christian's destiny. In everything Jesus is pre-eminent. 'God was pleased', continues the apostle, 'to have all his fullness dwell in him.' He repeats that claim later in 2:9: 'in Christ all the fulness of the Deity lives in bodily form.' You could hardly put it more strongly than that.

The Colossians in their syncretism were wanting to distribute what they called 'the fullness' among many 'thrones or powers or rules or authorities', but Paul maintains the fullness is to be found in Christ alone (2:9): 'In Christ all the fullness of the Deity lives in bodily form.' It would be hard to exaggerate the power of his claim. In Greek there are two words for 'lives' or 'dwells' and he uses the stronger one, meaning 'has its permanent home'. There are likewise two words for 'deity' – and once again Paul uses the strong word lest there should be any misapprehension on the part of his readers, or ourselves.

And finally he claims that it is in the historical Jesus that this divine incarnation has taken place 'bodily', i.e. 'by Christ's physical body'. It is difficult to imagine that anyone could have chosen words more clear and decisive. It is permissible to maintain that Paul was wrong: it is hard to claim that he is merely being poetic.

The other passage of Paul's is Philippians 2:5–11. It gives us a profound insight into what Paul means when he applies the word 'Lord' to Jesus. The word itself, *kyrios*, can mean anything from 'sir' to 'God almighty'. How are we to understand it when applied to Jesus? This passage gives the answer. It is almost universally recognized that Paul is here citing a very early Christian hymn. Indeed, it goes back easily into Aramaic, the language Jesus and the first Christians habitually spoke.

In these few verses we find a combination of three of the highest Old Testament motifs. Jesus is the Son of Man, colleague of the Ancient of Days (God), according to Daniel 7:13. He is the Suffering Servant of the Lord who bears the sins of the world, according to Isaiah 53. And supremely he takes the place of God Almighty in the Old Testament, as the one to whom every knee will bow and every tongue confess that Jesus is Lord (Isaiah 45:23). Is it not astonishing that within a few years of the death of this penniless carpenter his followers should be ransacking the Old Testament for titles to do justice to his person and significance? And is it not astonishing that they should settle on one which invited universal worship and loyalty, the name of God himself? That is the 'name above every name'. That is the name conferred on Jesus. That is what lies behind the word 'Lord' when applied to him. He is identified with almighty God who had said in Isaiah 45:22–23, 'I am God, and there is no other. By myself I have sworn, my mouth has uttered in all integrity a word that will not be revoked: Before me every knee will bow; by me every tongue will swear.' Mere poetry, do you think?

Of course such a claim does not mean that God Almighty has abdicated in favour of his Son. It does mean that the Son shares the Father's nature, and that the God to whom universal worship will be given is the one who has disclosed himself in Jesus. It would be ridiculous to say that Jesus is God *tout simple*. The New Testament writers do not claim this for him; they know he is also very much one of us. But they do insist that he is not just one of us. He is, so to speak, the window into God.

That is why Paul insists that before the incarnation Jesus shared the very form of God: 'who, being in very nature God, did not consider equality with God something to be grasped' (Philippians 2:6). That is another very careful bit of writing. There are two Greek words which express the participle 'being'. The weaker is *ōn*; the stronger, *huparchōn* (meaning 'being from the beginning'). And it is this stronger word which Paul uses when speaking of Jesus as being in the very nature (or form) of God. Again there are two words for 'form', and once again Paul chooses the stronger word, *morphē*, when he says Jesus was, from the very beginning, in the form of God.

So the meaning of this amazingly profound 'hymn' to Christ in Philippians 2 is this, in a nutshell. It means that Jesus had always been one with God; that he voluntarily laid aside those aspects of his Deity which would have been impossible to combine with our human condition; that he became one of us and shared our death, even death on a cross. That he was raised from the dead and the Father has bestowed on him the divine name to which every knee will eventually bow. A mind-boggling claim! But that is what the first Christians believed. And that is what Paul, the persecutor-turned-apostle believed, or he would not have quoted this ancient hymn.

I have spent some time on Paul partly because he is such an important witness and partly because he is probably the earliest writer we have in the New Testament. He wrote between twenty and thirty years after the crucifixion. He puts us in touch with the beliefs of the first Christians.

But the really significant thing is the way in which this conviction about Christ set out by Paul is to be found everywhere in the New Testament. Here are some examples.

The claims of the Gospel writers

Each of the four evangelists makes plain this conviction in his own way. Mark, the earliest, heads his work, 'The beginning of the gospel about Jesus Christ, the Son of God' (Mark

1:1), and at once introduces a trinitarian motif in the story of
the baptism of Jesus, where the voice of the Father and the
coming of the Spirit combine to assure Jesus (and the reader):
'You are my Son, whom I love; with you I am well pleased'
(1:11).

Matthew is at pains to draw attention both to the significance
of Jesus' name, which means 'God to the rescue' (see Matthew
1:21) and to the fact that his coming means 'Emmanuel',
'God with us' (1:23).

Luke introduces Jesus with the words, 'He will be great
and will be called the Son of the Most High. The Lord God
will give him the throne of his father David, and he will reign
over the house of Jacob for ever; his kingdom will never end.'
'The Holy Spirit will come upon you', so runs the message
to Mary his mother, 'and the power of the Most High will
overshadow you. So the holy one to be born will be called
the Son of God' (Luke 1:32–35).

John is the most explicit of all. He uses the title 'the Word'
which had strong connotations both in Hebrew thought and
in Greek philosophy. But he declares what no Greek philosopher, no Hebrew prophet would ever have dared to say
about anyone – that the Word, this incomparably superior
being who shared God's life, his creativity and his very nature,
became flesh and lived among us. There is no way we can
evade his plain meaning. He insists that this Word was in the
beginning with God. He is the principle of life. He is the agent
in creation. He is the light of the world. And he is God! Yet
he became flesh.

John is claiming that within the confines of a human life,
indeed of his personal friend, the Ultimate had become
embodied, the Absolute had become contemporary. It was
the strongest philosophical claim for the deity of Christ. And
when John continues to say (1:18), 'No one has ever seen God,

but God the One and Only, who is at the Father's side, has made him known', then the claim that Jesus was never seen as God before Nicea is shown up as the ludicrous lie which it is. Throughout the Gospel we find comments such as that Jesus 'was even calling God his Father, making himself equal with God' (5:18). We therefore are well prepared for Thomas' confession, when he falls in worship at the end of the book, 'My Lord and my God' (20:28). After all, the author explicitly claims that he has chosen to record incidents from the life of Jesus which will lead his readers to 'believe that Jesus is the Christ, the Son of God' (20:31). The evangelist believed it. He wanted others to believe it too.

One of the oldest parts of the Gospels is the material that we looked at earlier, known as Q, a substantial body of the sayings of Jesus recorded in Matthew and Luke but absent from Mark. Does the Q material embody this amazing claim to Deity which we find in the New Testament as a whole? Yes it does. There is a remarkable passage (in Matthew 11:25ff. with its parallel in Luke 10:21ff.) where Jesus claims a unique and exclusive relationship with the Father. He maintains that he alone knows the Father. He alone can introduce men and women to the Father. To him alone the Father has committed all things. And he is prepared to welcome anyone who comes to him. 'All things have been committed to me by my Father. No-one knows the Son except the Father, and no-one knows the Father except the Son and those to whom the Son chooses to reveal him. Come to me, all you who are weary and burdened, and I will give you rest.' What religious leader has ever spoke like that? These are the words of one who can point to himself with both humility and authority because he does in fact constitute the meeting point of God and humankind.

I do not want to labour the point. But there is one other passage in the New Testament which is so unequivocal that we must look at it. It comes at the very beginning of the letter to the Hebrews, written in the late sixties AD. 'In the past God spoke to our forefathers through the prophets at many times and in various ways, but in these last days he has spoken to us by his Son . . . ' A powerful contrast between prophets and Son, but could 'Son' be metaphorical language? See how the writer continues: ' . . . whom he appointed heir of all things, and through whom he made the universe. The Son is the radiance of God's glory and the exact representation of his being, sustaining all things by his powerful word' (Hebrews 1:1–3).

In other words, Jesus is God's final and personal message to humankind; beyond him, God has nothing more to say. He is the one for whom the whole world exists. He is the one who fashioned it. He sustains the whole universe. He reflects the nature of God (the Greek original hints that he does so as closely as sunshine reflects the sun). He bears the stamp of God's character – and the original hints that he does so as precisely as marks in the wax reflect the seal that made them.

Such is the conviction of the writer to the Hebrews. Such, in essence, however variously expressed, is the conviction of all the New Testament writers. They had come to the conclusion that in a unique, personal way, 'God was in Christ'. This was no exaggeration, no hyperbole, mythology or poetic licence. They believed that God had become incarnate.

The witness of the early Christians following the New Testament

That conviction of Jesus as God incarnate was there from the start and remained firm in the second and succeeding centuries. 'God himself was manifest in human form,' wrote the Christian bishop Ignatius, martyred about AD 107. And again, 'I pray for your happiness for ever in our God, Jesus Christ.'

The *Letter of Barnabas*,* which was probably written in the last quarter of the first century, speaks of 'the Son of God who is Lord of all things and will judge the living and the dead'. 'It is fitting that you should think of Jesus Christ as God,' wrote the distinguished theologian Clement, about AD 150. At much the same time the saintly bishop Polycarp speaks of 'Jesus Christ who is the Son of God and our everlasting High Priest'. Justin, the Christian philosopher writing about AD 140, affirms, 'Our Teacher is both Son and Apostle of God the Father of all, and the Ruler, Jesus Christ, from whom we have the name of Christians.' Again he writes, more succinctly, 'The Father of the universe has a Son. And he is God.' 'He is God, as his name Emmanuel indicates,' said Irenaeus, the greatest leader of the second century church (c. AD 180).

Wherever we look in the writings of the Christian church, from the earliest days, we find this fundamental conviction of the deity of Jesus Christ. That, after all, was the main charge brought against them by their opponents. That is why they were spasmodically persecuted by the Roman state. Christians refused to worship Caesar as God or Jupiter as God – they kept that name for somebody else.

Was there any precedent for seeing anyone as divine in the Hellenistic world?

We have seen that the New Testament and early Christian writers were united in ascribing deity to Jesus, and that they did not mean it in any attenuated, mythic or poetic sense. It is worth asking whether there was any precedent for so astonishing a claim in the Hellenistic world.

*Not to be confused with the medieval forgery, *The Gospel of Barnabas*, see p. 82.

At first sight there seem to be many parallels. The mystery cults are an obvious example. What if Jesus was called 'Lord' by his followers? So was Serapis. What if he was said to be born of a virgin? So were half the members of the pantheon. What if he was supposed to have ascended into heaven? So was Hercules, raised thereby to the rank of divinity; and so were the Roman emperors after their decease (it all began when someone claimed to have seen a new star arise from Julius Caesar's funeral pyre!). What was so special about Jesus?

The really special thing was this: nobody had ever attributed divinity and a virgin birth, resurrection and ascension, to a *historical person* whom lots of people knew. And certainly nobody had claimed that the one and only God, the Creator and Judge of the whole earth, had embodied himself in Apollo, Hercules, Augustus and the rest. Apollo and the others were mythical figures whom nobody in their right mind believed in; but they were there in Homer and were thus part of the culture of the Graeco-Roman world – and anyhow they furnished entertaining stories. Hercules and the like, born of the amours of Zeus and mortal women, were equally imaginary figures, one stage lower down; they were demigods, and if they reached the ranks of the Immortals it was not due so much to the accident of their birth as to the achievement of their lives.

As for the ruler cult, we have seen that it was a convenient tool to bind together a religiously, culturally and politically diverse empire. But of course neither Augustus who inaugurated the practice, nor his successors, imagined that by the imperial cult they were laying claim to embody the Godhead. Indeed, Augustus prides himself in his *Res Gestae* (a chronicle of his virtuous actions) for restoring the temples of the gods which had fallen on hard times during the previous century of civil war. No, if we wonder how seriously we should take the 'divinization' of the dying emperor, we do not have far to look. Seneca poked fun at the idea in his *Pumpkinification of Claudius* in the fifties, and Vespasian, dying in the seventies, quipped, 'Alas, I fear I am becoming a god.' It is very difficult to suppose that the Christian convictions about Jesus sprang from such roots.

But some have tried to make such a case! Early in the twentieth century, W. Bousset argued that the attribution of Lordship to Jesus arose on pagan soil, where, as Paul acknowledged, there were 'lords many'. His 'deification', in other words, took place under Hellenistic influences as the church spread. But to this there is a fatal objection. The title and the belief did not arise on pagan soil at all, but on monotheistic Jewish soil, the hardest place in the world for any such conviction to arise. We have its Aramaic original in the formula, *Maranatha* (1 Corinthians 16:22). Depending on how you divide the word up, it means either 'Our Lord has come' or the cry, 'O our Lord, come!' It either attests Christ's incarnation or looks for his return. But it certainly addresses Jesus as *mara*, 'Lord'. The Old Testament was of course written in Hebrew not Aramaic, but we have plenty of examples of the word *mara* as a title for God in the Aramaic inter-testamental literature that has come to light at Qumran. The last plank of the supposed derivation of the deity from pagan parallels has proved utterly untrustworthy.

Was there any precedent for seeing anyone as divine in Jewish circles?

Perhaps we shall have better luck when we turn to the Jewish sources. At first sight it is highly improbable that Judaism should offer any good parallels to the attribution of divine sonship to Jesus, because its creed was so unambiguously and jealously monotheistic. And the more you look at it, the stronger that first assumption proves to be.

Some have argued that Isaiah 7:14 indicates that the Jews were at least sympathetic to the idea of a virgin birth. By no means! Virgin births did not figure in the religious mindset of a Jew. He knew that *almah*, the word translated 'virgin' in that Isaiah passage, merely meant 'young woman', perhaps a virgin, perhaps not. Marriage, not virginity, was the Jewish ideal for women. Indeed Hebrew has no proper word for bachelor! And yet it is in this utterly unpromising Jewish soil that the story of Jesus' virginal conception, recorded in Matthew and Luke, complete with their Jewish phraseology and Jewish genealogies, grew up. We have already seen that these stories owe nothing to supposed parallels with pagan stories of intercourse between the gods and human women. No, the birth stories are without analogy in either pagan or Jewish literature, like the rest of the material which goes to make up the New Testament claim that, in Jesus, God was present in our world.

To be sure, the king had long been called 'the son of God' in an emasculated, adoptionist and figurative sense (see for example, Psalm 2:7). Ancient worthies such as Enoch invited speculation about their ascension to God – for did not the biblical text say, enigmatically, 'And Enoch walked with God; then he was no more, because God took him away' (Genesis 5:24)? Philosophers like Philo in Alexandria might seek to commend Judaism to a Hellenistic culture by speaking of the Law as personified Wisdom or pre-cosmic Reason (the Logos) but all this is poles apart from the explicit, unambiguous claim of the many writers who go to make up the New Testament, that Jesus was metaphysically, not metaphorically, one with God Almighty.

Dan Brown claims that Jesus was hailed as divine only at the Council of Nicea. But we have seen that claim is a lie. He was seen as divine from the very start of Christianity, when they still spoke Aramaic and were viewed merely as a strange group within Judaism. All the New Testament writers saw him as divine in the fullest sense, and so did their successors in the period after the apostles. There is no precedent in either Jewish or pagan sources for regarding a human being, whom lots of people knew, as sharing the nature of Almighty God the Creator, Saviour and Judge of the world.

Appropriately, therefore, the earliest Christians devised the symbol of a fish to denote their allegiance. The Greek letters which make up the word 'fish' stand for 'Jesus Christ, Son of God, Saviour'. And that was the unique, fearless and unequivocal conviction of Christians, not after the Council of Nicea, but from the very beginning.

11. 'THE "NEW" TESTAMENT IS EVIL'

So far we have looked at particular attacks on Jesus. But in his recent book, *God is not Great*, Christopher Hitchens, a swashbuckling journalist and one of the foremost protagonists of the 'New Atheism', launches a caustic broadside against all religion, including of course Christianity. He does not aim a rifle at it, with one bullet, but a shotgun with a large number of pellets in each cartridge! So it is not possible within the limits of this one chapter to respond to all the points he makes, particularly the many throwaway insults. Instead I will concentrate on the chapter in his book in which he deals most directly with Jesus, called, 'The Evil of the "New" Testament'. It immediately follows 'The nightmare of the "Old" Testament', so we can guess what we are in for!

His basic premise in approaching the New Testament is that it is totally unreliable. Its authors are 'ignorant' and 'illiterate'. It is 'a work of crude carpentry, hammered together long after its purported events, and full of improvised attempts to make things come out right'. He cites with approval a very influencial American writer of the first half of the twentieth century, H. L. Mencken, who 'irrefutably' claims: 'The simple fact is that the New Testament as we know it is a helter-skelter of more or less discordant documents, some of them probably of respectable origin, but others palpably apocryphal and most of them, the good along with the bad, show unmistakable signs of having been tampered with.'

Has the text of the New Testament been tampered with?

It is difficult to reply to such undocumented and unspecific allegations, but two of them need a summary response. Hitchens maintains both that the New Testament documents were put together long after its purported events, and that the documents show unmistakable signs of having been tampered with. As we have seen in chapters five and six, both claims are without foundation. On the integrity of the New Testament text, Hitchens pays undue attention to Bart Ehrman, an American New Testament scholar who has moved from fundamentalism to atheism, and so he suits Hitchens' purposes admirably. Ehrman says that he lost his faith through postgraduate work on the text of the New Testament.

He became very worried by the amount of variant readings it contains. But as we have already seen, variant readings are inevitable if you have no printing and are dictating the text to amateur scribes, which was the situation with the New Testament. Actually, anyone who has seen some of these ancient manuscripts personally can only be amazed at the skill and care with which they were transcribed: but yes, there are many small variations. This is entirely natural considering we have some 24,000 ancient manuscripts of the New Testament in various languages, compared with ten of Caesar, seven of Plato and twenty of Tacitus. Most of the variants are entirely trivial, often with only a single letter being in doubt.

The truth of the matter is that there is no body of ancient literature in the world that enjoys such a wealth of good textual attestation as the New Testament. No single Christian doctrine is affected by any uncertainty in the text. And as pointed out in chapter five, only two serious questions arise about any portion of the text.

The first is the ending of Mark's Gospel. Did he intend to end it at chapter 16, verse 8, or was the gospel unfinished for some reason – perhaps the death or the arrest of the author? This is an open question, extensively debated by New Testament scholars. Verses 9–20 were added by a later hand, and no scholars that I am aware of deny it. It is a summarizing conclusion, added by some very early Christian, perhaps Aristeas, as one manuscript attests. But every first-year theology undergraduate knows that. It is not a cause for losing your faith. And it is certainly not the case as Hitchens (ignorantly) says, that one of Ehrman's 'more astonishing discoveries is that the account of Jesus' resurrection in the Gospel of Mark was only added many years later'. If he means that it was Ehrman who discovered that Mark 16:9–20 was post-Marcan, this was no discovery at all: everybody involved in New Testament study has known it for ages. If he means that Ehrman 'discovered' that there is nothing about the resurrection in the Gospel of Mark, this is rubbish. The resurrection is clearly attested in the end of the unquestioned Gospel of Mark. Verses 6–7 say:

> 'Don't be alarmed,' he said. 'You are looking for Jesus the Nazarene, who was crucified. He has risen! He is not here. See the place where they laid him. But go, tell his disciples and Peter, "He is going ahead of you into Galilee. There you will see him, just as he told you."'

We have already mentioned the other passage which is insecure in the textual tradition, the story of Jesus and the woman caught in the act of adultery. It is true that some of the earliest and best manuscripts omit it. But many others include it, either in its traditional place in John 7:53 – 8:11, or after John 7:36 or Luke 21:38. What are we to make of this?

The most probable explanation is this. The story unquestionably breathes the spirit of Jesus, his repudiation of hypocrisy, his free forgiveness, and his challenge to transformation. The story will have circulated for a while independently, like many others which got gathered into the Gospels. Preachers would have used it to illustrate the way Jesus forgives sinners along with his demand for a change of lifestyle. It was inserted into the Gospels because it was too precious to jettison, but scribes were uncertain where to put it.

Needless to say, no Christian doctrine and no major historical truth depends on either of these disputed passages. We could make a gift of both of them to Christopher Hitchens with our best wishes, and that would not alter the case for the historicity of the New Testament at all.

Are the New Testament accounts inaccurate and self-contradictory?

That is the claim of Mr Hitchens. 'Their multiple authors – none of whom published anything until decades after the crucifixion – cannot agree on anything of importance. Matthew and Luke cannot concur on the Virgin Birth or the genealogy of Jesus.' Let's have a look at some of the examples he adduces in support of his claim.

The census
He brings up the old problem ('fabrication' he calls it) about Quirinius and the census. Luke 2:1 tells us that this was 'the first census', taken when Quirinius was governor of Syria. This well known census was in 6 AD when the Romans took

over Judea, and it provoked a violent uprising. However Luke has invariably proved to be precise when he speaks of Roman provincial administration or the titles of officials, and he is well aware of that census in AD 6, for he refers to it in Acts 5:37, so it is gratuitous to suppose he is a decade out here, since Jesus must have been born before the death of Herod the Great in 4 BC. We know that the emperor Augustus was very particular about conducting censuses within the empire and imposing taxes. He wrote in his own hand a *breviarium totius imperii* which gave 'the number of the citizens and of allies under arms, of the fleets, of the kingdoms, of the provinces, and of the tributes or taxes'. Herod ran Judea as a client kingdom, and would have had to impose the census of Luke 2:1 at Augustus' request. And because, coming from Herod, it looked like domestic legislation, it would not have provoked the fury of the 'first census' conducted by Rome when she came in as conquering pagan power to take over the province, in AD 6.

There are several possible ways of taking Luke's words in 2:1ff.. The Greek can be translated 'the enrolment was earlier than that held when Quirinius was governor of Syria'. Another possibility is this. The first century *lapis Tiburtinus* refers to a (most unusual) second proconsulship of Syria, held by someone whose name is unfortunately broken off, but the other details recorded on it all fit Quirinius. If so, there is no problem about the date given by Luke – it would refer to Quirinius' earlier appointment. We know that he spent most of his official career in Syria-Palestine.

Another possibility is that the word translated 'governor' may refer not to proconsular power but to military command, and we know Quirinius conducted extensive campaigns against the Homanadenses between 10 and 7 BC (during which period Jesus was probably born), while the civil administration of the province was in the hands of other governors, including Sentius Saturninus (8–6 BC) under whom, according to Tertullian, the census of Luke 2:1ff. was held. So although there is as yet no certainty about the matter, Hitchens has no justification in roundly asserting that Luke just got it wrong.

Other 'mistakes'

Hitchens claims that the evangelists 'disagree wildly on the Sermon on the Mount, the anointing of Jesus, the treachery of Judas and Peter's haunting denial'. How do those claims stand up?

Matthew and Luke do not disagree wildly on the Sermon on the Mount. Both begin with the Beatitudes and end with the parables of two houses. The whole of Luke's material is found in Matthew, but Matthew is concerned to group the teaching of Jesus into five great blocks, to parallel the five books of Moses and show that Jesus is the new Moses. He combines the sermon as it appeared in the saying-source Q (common both to him and Luke) with other material drawn from different parts of Q. There is no violent disagreement: merely selection of material, such as Mr Hitchens himself does so expertly.

There are in fact no conflicts between the accounts of the treachery of Judas to be found in the Gospels, though John has access to more information about it than the synoptics do. There is no discrepancy either, in the story of Jesus' anointing.

Matthew and Mark tell of a supper party shortly before Jesus' death, at Bethany in the house of one Simon the leper. An unnamed woman comes and anoints his head, and it is interpreted as an anticipation of his burial. Judas, the treasurer of the disciples, complains at this 'waste' of the precious ointment which could have realized a big price. Luke does not record this story. However he does know of another, quite different anointing. Jesus was having a meal in a Pharisee's house at some unspecified time during his Galilean ministry. A 'woman who had lived a sinful life' slips into the dinner party and weeps, dries his feet with her hair and then anoints them with precious ointment. The Pharisee says to himself, 'If this man were a prophet, he would know who is touching him and what kind of woman she is – that she is a sinner' (Luke 7:39). Jesus points out that the woman has made up for the host's lack of the normal courtesies of hospitality, and that the tears and anointing are palpable marks of her repentance for her sins and her gratitude to the one who has forgiven them.

There is little similarity in the stories, less still in their contexts, and once again Hitchens is gratuitously imputing wild divergence where there is none at all!

The virgin birth

Hitchens has no time for the virgin birth without, of course, examining the testimony to it. He wrongly imagines that Matthew's belief in it (Matthew 1:23) was based on mis-understanding *almah* in Isaiah 7:14 to necessitate the meaning of 'virgin' rather than 'young woman' – the word can mean either. In point of fact, Matthew knew his Hebrew very well, and, like all Jews, he had a very high regard for the Old Testament.

On no less than twelve occasions, of which this is one, Matthew sees some aspect of Jesus' birth, ministry and death as a fulfilment of what was foreshadowed or even hinted at in the Old Testament. Some of these Old Testament refer-ences have to be somewhat strained to refer to Jesus at all! But this merely shows that the 'Jesus event' is primary and the Old Testament allusion secondary.

Matthew knows the Old Testament is inspired: he also knows Jesus is the fullest expression of God's revelation. Therefore, Matthew reckons, there has to be a correlation between the two. And here Matthew sees the virgin conception of Jesus as primary, and the supporting reference to Isaiah 7:14 about the *almah* as secondary. This is clear not only from the straightforward account itself (Matthew 1:18–25) but also from the way he casts the genealogy of Jesus. He specifically changes his repeated 'X was the father of Y' pattern, because he knows it was not so in the case of Jesus. He writes 'Mary, of whom [singular] was born Jesus, who is called Christ'.

Matthew was a strong believer in the unity of revelation and presents Jesus as the climax of all God's revelation in the Old Testament. But that was not the source of his confident belief in the virgin conception, which is independently attested by Luke, by the apostle Paul, and arguably by Mark.

To return to Hitchens, he dismisses the two genealogies of Jesus in Matthew and Luke, with no recognition that the one in Matthew is tracing the genealogy of Joseph, Jesus' legal father, while that in Luke is tracing the descent of Mary, Jesus' actual mother. Both of them came from Davidic descent. There is nothing surprising in the preservation of genealogies: Jews of that period majored on them. Thus Gamaliel, the tutor of the apostle Paul, could trace his parentage back to David.

Hitchens laughs at the star of Bethlehem without realizing that there was a conjunction of Jupiter and Saturn in the area of the sky known as Pisces three times in the year 6 BC, which was very probably the year in which Jesus was born. This astral event is attested by cuneiform tablets of astrologers found at Sippar in Babylonia, and the conjunction would have looked like a single very bright star. This extremely rare event

(I gather it did not occur again until noted by Kepler in 1603) was highly significant. Jupiter was the royal star, Saturn the star of the Jews, and Pisces indicated change. This would be more than enough to motivate learned astrologers to go to Judea to see if they could find the one to whom this portent referred.

And so we might go on. It is one thing to throw out random accusations. It is quite another to validate them.

The church and the coming of the kingdom

Two more substantial points which Hitchens raises are the failure of the second coming to materialize, and Jesus' 'complete indifference to the founding of any temporal church'. These are points worth examining briefly.

One of the notable features in Jesus' teaching about the coming of the kingdom is this. Whereas Jewish expectation looked for a single, unified break-in of God's kingly rule, Jesus split that eschatological expectation into two. A careful study of the Gospels reveals that at times Jesus speaks of the kingdom of God as present or having arrived, and at times he sees it as future when the Son of Man (as he called himself) would come back to this world in glory. It is often held that he taught, and the disciples expected, this to take place during their lifetime. That may well have been their expectation, but it was not his teaching.

The most celebrated verses on the subject are Mark 13:32–33. While predicting the fall of Jerusalem (which took place forty years later) and maintaining that his own teaching would never pass away (it hasn't!) Jesus says, 'No one knows of that day or hour, not even the angels in heaven, nor the Son, but only the Father.' He is speaking of his return in glory. Here is a verse that should pass the scrutiny even of

Mr Hitchens – something Jesus says he does not know! It is recognized as a mark of authenticity even among the Jesus Seminar. Elsewhere Jesus indicates that he will return like a thief in the night – nobody knows when. It was a saying that reverberated round the early church (Matthew 24:42–44; Luke 12:39–40; 1 Thessalonians 5:2; 2 Peter 3:10; Revelation 3:3). There was no excuse for anyone in that first generation complaining that Jesus had not returned in his or her lifetime. He himself had said he did not know when it would be. So the 'glaring' mistake on the time of his second coming turns out to be nothing of the sort.

But did Jesus intend to found a church? At first sight he does not seem to say much about it. But look a little closer and you will find the matter is different. There are explicit verses, such as Matthew 16:18. Peter has just made the climactic confession of Jesus as Messiah and Son of God, and Jesus responds by saying that on this rock he will build his 'church'. In Matthew 18:17 Jesus refers disputes to his 'church' for settlement. There is a similar thought in Luke 12:32: 'Do not be afraid, little flock, for your Father has been pleased to give you the kingdom.' The Twelve were his 'little flock'.

Jesus' appeal was to Israel as a whole to return in allegiance to the God who had directed their history over the centuries. But as opposition hardened, it was obvious that not all Israel would respond, and so Jesus increasingly committed himself to the Twelve (a significant number, by the way, reflecting the twelve tribes of Israel, and perhaps indicating the foundation of the new Israel). And at the end of his life he commissioned his followers to go into all the world and make disciples. If all that shows indifference to the founding of a church, words do not mean anything. Hitchens' journalistic generalizations have no substance.

Is the atonement immoral?

Hitchens points out that in various religions the offering of a human sacrifice is deemed appropriate for appeasing the gods. He sees that in the cross, too, there is a vicarious atonement: 'Once again we have a father demonstrating love by subjecting his son to death by torture, but this time the father is not trying to impress god. He is god, and he is trying to impress humans.'

Hitchens proceeds to reflect critically on the morality of the Christian account of the atonement. He personally would not have wanted Jesus to die in such agony had he been there: he would have tried to stop it. Christian teaching invites him to acknowledge that he is responsible for the flogging and mocking of the crucifixion, though of course he was not there. He is required to believe that it was necessary in order to compensate for an earlier crime in which he had no part, the sin of Adam. And if he uses his free will to reject the story, he is faced with an 'eternity of torture more awful than anything endured at Calvary'. There is certainly a case here to be answered, even though it rests upon some misconceptions.

The most important thing to say to Christopher Hitchens is this. It is quite wrong to think of God the Father taking it out of his Son on behalf of sinful human beings. He is indeed God but he is not trying to impress humans. He is willingly entering into our most profound plight, our alienation from himself. Far from torturing his Son, *God was in Christ*, reconciling the world to himself – so reads the New Testament (2 Corinthians 5:19). And that puts a very different complexion on it, does it not? Would you not be profoundly grateful if someone cared enough about you to go broke himself in order to pay your debts? If someone was willing to break his back carrying a load that was too heavy for you? Make no mistake about it. That load was incredibly heavy. Our thoughts, words, deeds, our addictions, our characters add up to an unclean load by which no God worthy of the name could fail to be repulsed. And the teaching of the New Testament is that God was repulsed by the concentrated evil of humankind and yet loved us enough to take the responsibility for it himself.

Of course, Calvary cannot liquidate the evil that I do to myself by addictive or destructive behaviour. It cannot liquidate the evil that I do to other people whom I harm. But surely it *can* liquidate the responsibility before a holy God that inevitably accompanies my actions. God can accept me, and even acquit me, knowing that he has himself dealt with the accusing charge against me. There is nothing immoral in that. There is no idea that a vengeful Father punishes an innocent Son for guilty you and me. The cross is perfectly moral, perfectly fair and perfectly loving. Such is the God we worship. No other God would be worth worshipping.

But there are other misunderstandings in the scenario Hitchens has sketched. They are worth examining, because many people share them. He seems to think that he is deemed personally 'responsible for the flogging and mocking and crucifixion, in which I had no say and no part'. You cannot be responsible for what you have not done (or failed to do). But you can be caught up in the entail of it. Thus a youngster is not *responsible* for the drunken violence in which his father engaged, but he is *affected* by it. Christian teaching does not make Hitchens responsible for the physical actions which led to the actual crucifixion of Jesus. But it does proclaim loud and clear that Hitchens is part of the flawed humanity for whose redemption Jesus died.

Hitchens seems fixated on this misunderstanding. He thinks, 'I am required to believe that the agony [of the cross] was necessary in order to compensate for an earlier crime in which I also had no part, the sin of Adam . . . My own guilt in the matter is deemed "original" and inescapable.' He has taken on board a somewhat garbled understanding of Augustine on original sin.

In essence, the point is this. You cannot get clean water out of a dirty river. That is what 'original sin' is all about. And Hitchens, together with all the rest of us, has been imbibing dirty water all his life. He, like the rest of us, is stained with the wrongdoing that has, from earliest times, marked all human beings. So yes, we are all *affected* by the sin of Adam, if you like to put it that way. But we are not *responsible* for it. We are accountable for our own actions, and responsible for our own wrongdoings and failures to do right. As I look back on mine, I confess that they are weighty enough in all conscience. They cut me off from awareness of God, let alone from communion with God. That is what the cross set out to rectify.

Hitchens confuses original sin with original guilt. He writes, 'my own guilt in the matter is deemed "original" and inescapable'. Not so. We can only be held guilty for our own responsible actions and failures. And the glory of the gospel is that God is big enough, just enough and self-sacrificing enough to have handled those failures on our behalf. The cost of so doing was truly agonizing. But it means that free acceptance is open to all.

That, too, sticks in Hitchens' throat. After the complaint we have just been examining, he continues: 'However I am still granted free will with which to reject the offer of vicarious redemption. Should I exercise this choice, however, I face an eternity of torture much more awful than anything endured at Calvary, or anything threatened to those who first heard Ten Commandments.'

Here is another misconception – that 'an eternity of torture' awaits those who decline the offer of God's salvation.

That is, however, only one of three possible Christian views about the future. None of them is empirically verifiable until we get there, and in any case we are told not to judge, because that is God's prerogative, not ours.

One of the three is indeed conscious unending torment for those who deliberately reject the gospel. Many popular presentations of this view, such as that put by Hitchens, seem to owe much of their content to modern horror films and ancient poems like Virgil's *Aeneid* or Dante's *Inferno*.

The second view is that we human beings are a psycho-somatic unity, with full physical and mental life, and the potential for a life with God for ever. If we decline to actualize that potential, we shall indeed miss out on it. But that is not because God is mean and refuses to welcome us. It is because, if we die unrepentant, we have turned our backs on that relationship with God which is eternal life. God will not have conscripts in his heaven. The Bible does indeed speak not only of 'eternal life' but of 'everlasting destruction . . . shut out from the presence of the Lord'. It means irreversible destruction: we miss out on what we were made for. But it does not involve 'an eternity of torture': but rather annihilation.

There is a third view which has had considerable currency among Christians, and still does. It is that in the end the sheer magnetism of God's love will bring all of us rebels to throw away our arms of refusal: in the end, all will be saved. This view is much harder to reconcile with the teaching of Jesus: however, fortunately we are not required to judge between these alternatives! But all of them have been, and are held, by believing Christians, and all of them have some root in the New Testament. Mr Hitchens need not be kept back by a Virgilian view of hell from accepting the wonderful reconciliation held out to him by the God of whom this 'evil' New Testament speaks.

I have spent considerable time on this accusation that the atonement is immoral, because it goes to the very heart of Christianity. This means that I have inevitably had to spend less time on other accusations and errors made by Mr Hitchens. But I have kept one of them to the end because it is egregious. He alludes to the Gnostic gospels found near Nag Hammadi in Egypt. They have elicited a lot of interest in recent years. He says, 'These scrolls were of the same period and provenance as many of the subsequently canonical and "authorized Gospels".' As we saw in chapter two this is an astonishing and very ignorant misreading of the evidence.

The Gnostic gospels do not have the same provenance as the canonical Gospels: they originated in Egypt, not Palestine. They are not of the same period, but two hundred years later. And the Gospels we have in the New Testament were not 'subsequently canonical and authorized', but from the first century itself were recognized without argument in the early church as its foundation documents, putting subsequent believers in touch with the historical Jesus, his teaching and his disciples. Three major errors in one sentence! Mr Hitchens will have to do better than this if he is to fulfil his aim of eradicating Christianity. And, incidentally, he could well adopt a less caustic and sneering tone. It does nothing to help his cause.

Dubious ethics in the teaching of Jesus?

Allow me to conclude this chapter by addressing a somewhat similar approach made by Sam Harris, another of the new atheists, in his book *Letter to a Christian Nation*. He is much more balanced and restrained in his accusations than Hitchens, and as a result his impact is likely to prove a good deal more persuasive. I shall not deal with much of his short book since it does not major on our topic of slurs against Jesus. But in one area it does. Beginning on page 8, he discusses the very tough penalties Deuteronomy lays down for the person who 'secretly entices you, saying, "Let us go and worship other gods" (gods that neither you nor your fathers have known, gods of the peoples around you, whether near or far, from one end of the land to the other), do not yield to him or listen to him. Show him no pity. Do not spare him or shield him. You must certainly put him to death. Your hand must be the first in putting him to death, and then the hands of all the people. Stone him to death, because he tried to turn you away from the LORD your God, who brought you out of Egypt, out of the land of slavery.'

Harris continues quoting from Deuteronomy 13 a little more and then says, 'Many Christians believe that Jesus did away with all this barbarism in the clearest terms imaginable and delivered a doctrine of pure love and toleration. He didn't. In fact at several points in the New Testament Jesus can be read to endorse the entirety of the Old Testament law.' He then turns for evidence to Matthew 5:18: 'I tell you the truth, until heaven and earth disappear, not the smallest letter, not the least stroke of a pen, will by any means disappear from the Law until everything is accomplished.' I suppose this just *could* be read as an endorsement of the tough punishments of the Old Testament. But that is not at all the most natural way to take it.

In this famous Sermon on the Mount from which Harris makes his quotation, there is absolutely nothing to suggest Jesus is endorsing the punitive laws of the Old Testament. That is not what it is about. The sermon begins with a description of the 'blessed life', one of the most beautiful moral challenges that has ever come from human lips. Jesus continues by urging his followers to shine like light in society, and to be like salt – which was a preservative against corruption. That doesn't sound much like encouraging people to stone others to death, does it? It is only after this that Jesus utters the words Harris quotes. He explains that he has not come to abolish or rubbish the Old Testament law, but rather to fulfil it. He goes on to intensify the morals of the Old Testament. Where it said, 'You shall not murder', Jesus traces that evil beast of murder to its lair in the human heart, anger. Where it said, 'You shall not commit adultery', Jesus intensifies it by tracing the evil of adultery back to the evil of lust in the heart.

What Jesus is doing in the sermon is to intensify the challenge of God's requirements. It is not only actions but attitudes that God wants cleansed. That is why Jesus tells his hearers that unless their righteousness exceeds that of the scribes and Pharisees they would never enter the kingdom of heaven. And what was that pharisaic righteousness? It was the attitude which said, 'I have obeyed what is required. I have been there, got the T-shirt and so God owes me one.' That attitude is repugnant. What God wants to see is the theme which concludes this fifth chapter of Matthew. 'You have heard that it was said, "Love your neighbour and hate your enemy." But I tell you: Love your enemies and pray for those who persecute you, that you may be sons of your Father in heaven.' And he urges them to show perfect love to all, and thus reflect the character of their heavenly Father.

It would be hard to imagine any passage being more unlike the one in Deuteronomy with which Harris began his critique. To be sure, the penalty of death by stoning is exceedingly tough. But notice what it was for: rejecting the Lord who brought them out of the bondage of Egypt and running off to serve other gods. Obedience in the Old Testament is never due to an arbitrary whim of God. It is his plea to those whom he has rescued. The ethics of the Old Testament and the New all spring from gratitude.

There is of course a gradation in those ethical standards, as God's people develop. As we saw in Matthew 5, Jesus intensifies them and looks not just for the external action but for the inner attitude. But back in the days of Deuteronomy God was trying to fashion a nation that would honour and serve him. A nation where in due course he could come and show his hand fully, as he did in the person of Jesus Christ. And if that nation had capitulated to other gods, if apostasy had run riot and gone unpunished, how could God's rescue plan for humanity ever have been accomplished? So drastic measures were needed.

It is rather like getting cancer in your body. Surgery is the only hope. The diseased part must be cut out. And that is what the tough laws of Deuteronomy were insisting on. They were necessary for their time.

We have to remind Sam Harris that the Romans had taken away the right of execution from their Jewish subjects long before Jesus came teaching, so it is ridiculous to suppose that he was supporting the stoning of which Deuteronomy speaks. On the contrary you find no hint of his showing violence to others. Rather, he willingly endured the role of innocent suffering, and absorbed its horror as he went to the cross, crying, 'Father, forgive them, for they do not know what they are doing.'

Sam Harris then appears to moderate his criticism of Jesus' ethics by admitting, 'Jesus said some profound things about love and charity and forgiveness. The Golden Rule is a wonderful moral precept.' There, wasn't that very generous of Harris? Not at all. He gives with one hand and takes back with the other, for he continues, 'But numerous teachers offered the same instruction centuries before Jesus (Zoroaster,

Buddha, Confucius, Epictetus).' Whoops! Centuries before Christ? Epictetus lived after him!

But it is quite true that there are partial parallels to the Golden Rule elsewhere. Harris mentions Confucius, and he is a good example. When asked for a one-word rule of life Confucius replied, 'Is not reciprocity such a word? What you do not want done to yourself, do not do to others.' An admirable precept. You can even enact a law to bring that about. Several countries have in fact done so. But you cannot do that with *the positive form* of the Golden Rule which, as far as we know, is unique to Jesus.

You can never legislate to bring about what Jesus is teaching – the overflow of love. The generous attitude of going out of your way to encourage the depressed, to forgive those who have wronged you, to meet need where you see it – all this requires action, and often sacrificial action. You don't do that to fulfil some law. You do it only if the love of the kingdom of God burns in you your heart. It is one thing to say, 'I must not harm my fellows.' It is quite another to say, 'I must go out of my way to help them.' The first could be fulfilled by inaction. The second only by sacrificial love – the very thing God showed by bringing people into his kingdom in the first place.

The truth of the matter is that if you could improve on the ethics of Jesus, it would require more than a *Letter to a Christian Nation*. It would make headline news in most of the papers of the world.

12. THE REAL TROUBLE WITH SCEPTICISM ABOUT THE JESUS STORY

Reflection on miracle and overtly supernatural elements in the Gospel records inevitably raises the issue of contemporary scepticism. It is commonplace to assume that it is the Christians who need to be defensive about their faith. However, the case for the reliability of the Gospels is very strong, whereas many of the sceptical attacks on it turn out, on inspection, to be unpersuasive. So it will be worth while examining some of the positions put forward by sceptics and see if they hold water. There are a number of objections that can be brought against the widespread historical scepticism we meet today in some scholars, and in a mass of popular books which depend on them. And the whole opposition to the miraculous is based on a highly questionable assumption, that God, if he exists, does not interfere within his world.

Sceptics make some strange assumptions

The first assumption made by sceptics runs something like this. All the records about Jesus that we have, come from after Easter. They are therefore all prejudiced since their authors wrote from the perspective of the Easter faith.

There is a logical fallacy within what might otherwise be a rather helpful observation. The authors did write from a conviction about the resurrection. But just because they held a point of view it does not mean that they were wrong! It is one thing to recognize bias and allow for it. It is quite another to suppose that because people passionately believe something to be true it must therefore be false! As a matter of fact, the readiness with which many of the sayings attributed to Jesus go back into Aramaic, and the features of his teaching which are without parallel in the life of the early church (such as his use of parables and the title, 'Son of Man'), indicate that we probably have elements in the Gospel tradition that antedate the dawning of their Easter faith. But even if we had none, it would not necessarily follow that a single word of the Gospel material was untrustworthy. It might be: it might not be. That would have to be established on quite other criteria.

A second strange assumption, advocated by sceptical scholars like Dennis Nineham, is that the early Christians had no interest in history, and therefore that nothing could have survived about Jesus unless it was useful for the preaching, worship or ethics of the early church. But why so extraordinary an assumption? Is it not in the highest degree probable that new Christians would want to know more about who this Jesus was, where and when he operated, and what he said? The danger of this sort of gratuitous assumption is that what looks like pieces of historical evidence in the Gospels are airily and illicitly dismissed.

A third unwarranted assumption is that the early church made up a great many of the stories in the Gospels and Acts. They did so, we are told, in order to 'historicize the myth of Jesus' or to meet their own requirements in areas like teaching and lifestyle. I find this sort of claim most unconvincing.

For one thing, it attributes enormous creative powers to the nameless 'community' of early Christians who are supposed to have made these stories up. But this is to neglect one of the most obvious facts of life: communities do not create! When we meet crisp, vibrant stories such as we find galore in the Gospels, is it not infinitely more probable that

168 | LIES, LIES, LIES!

they derive from a single gifted storyteller than from some nameless group of Hellenistic Christians?

For another, it neglects the fact that the early Christians were quite capable of distinguishing between their own teaching and that of Jesus, and they were meticulous in so doing (see the apostle Paul in 1 Corinthians 7:10, 25). What is more, if this account of the creative activity of the early church were correct, we should expect to find in the stories made up and attributed to Jesus the sort of issues that they themselves were concerned about – like baptism, the inclusion of Gentiles, and the Holy Spirit. These things are conspicuous by their absence. As Professor Richard Hanson puckishly commented, 'Why should this large collection of fictitious material have been composed by a number of anonymous authors within a few years of the death of this person whose existence was historical but about whom we can know nothing else historical in spite of four narratives which purport to tell us about him?'

Sceptics tend to neglect the judgment of ancient historians

One of the unfortunate facts in contemporary Gospel studies is that not many of those engaged in it have a thorough grounding in the disciplines of historical study. Few are expert in classical Greek or ancient history, let alone ancient historiography. This might not matter so much if they listened to those who were. But this is just what does not happen. One might suppose that scepticism about the historical Jesus might come from historians who had studied him with care. But nothing could be further from the truth. It is the theologians who are willing to dispense with historicity and the historians who are trying to restrain them! Distinguished ancient historians like Ramsay, Rostovtzeff, Henderson, Sherwin-White, ascribe a very high degree of reliability to the New Testament narratives. The same is true of New Testament scholars like Reicke, Staudinger, Stauffer, Moule, Hemer, Bruce and N. T. Wright, who have come to the New Testament after extensive classical studies. In other words, the historical scepticism is not induced by the material itself, but by the presuppositions of sceptical theologians and their followers.

Thus Oxford's outstanding classical scholar A. N. Sherwin-White expressed his amazement that when we have four near-contemporary accounts of the life of Jesus, theologians should distrust them, when it is so different in the case of Jesus' best known contemporary, the emperor Tiberius. We have four accounts of him, too, and not only are they written much later, but they differ wildly in what they say. But even this does not mean that it is impossible to know anything about the man or his life!

Sceptics fail to take account of the Jewishness of the New Testament

Sceptics like Robert Price and other members of the Jesus Seminar constantly assume that the church dreamed up stories about Jesus once Christianity had moved out into the Gentile world. The Christians, we are told, were influenced by pagan religious imagination, and Hellenistic myths. But this approach neglects two vital factors. One was the hatred Jews had of the Hellenistic culture and their determination to remain unspotted by it. The other was the retentiveness of the oriental memory. Many Jews knew the whole of the Pentateuch by heart, just as many Greeks could recite the whole of the Iliad. Teaching in school was done by means of repetition. The sheer power of memory which they possessed is hard for us to recapture in the age of the book and the television screen. But it existed, and to discount it is bad scholarship.

Even today old people can accurately recall events in their youth. I can remember much of the content of Churchill's wartime speeches to which I listened when I was a boy sixty years ago, and I do not have a particularly good memory. Are we to suppose that his contemporaries could not remember the teaching of a greater than Churchill thirty or so years later, despite the retentiveness of their memories?

It is important to bear in mind the sheer Jewishness of the New Testament. I am not merely pointing to the controlling effect on the possible vagaries of tradition imposed by the survival of eyewitnesses, but to the fact that they were Jews. The New Testament, though written in Greek, is not a Hellenistic book. Its greatest affinities lie with Judaism. Jesus was a Jewish rabbi, and the disciples were Jewish to a man. They had been educated in remembering the words of their master, and there is good reason to suppose that they were competent in recalling it accurately. (See Richard Bauckham's powerful book, *Jesus and the Eyewitnesses*.)

Sceptics frequently make gross errors in methodology

It is common for sceptical scholars to assert that if there is any parallel to a Gospel incident in the Old Testament, rabbinic Judaism, or the early church, then we must assume that the Christians made the story up, and it must be discounted. What a laughable idea!

Take the story of Jesus' temptations, for example. Just because the Jews spent forty years in the wilderness after their exodus from Egypt it does not mean that Jesus could not have spent forty days in the desert being tempted. A basic methodological error. Anyhow, how often do you say something totally original? Much of our talk relates to past events, and no doubt much of Jesus' talk reflects the history and teaching of the Old Testament. It would be very surprising if not, since the Jews lived on it. And if the first Christians are found doing something which is also told of Jesus, perhaps they were just obeying his commands!

There is of course some value in this so-called 'criterion of dissimilarity' but there are major weaknesses as well. It assumes we know enough about what could have been said by the early church or contemporary Judaism to distinguish it with certainty from the teaching of Jesus. We do not. In any case, this principle, if rigorously applied, would have two crazy consequences. It would only give us what is unique in the teaching of Jesus, which might lead to a very distorted picture of him. And it would rule out all continuity between the teacher and his disciples: it would mean that nothing Jesus taught them ever stuck!

Often you find sceptical writers comparing Gospel stories about Jesus to Norse or Homeric legends. Not an impressive analogy, since the latter took centuries to coalesce and the Gospels could only have had thirty years or less. In any case, the Gospel stories are very unlike pagan legends. One of the experts most at home in this sort of literature was the Oxford English don, C. S. Lewis. He comments robustly in *Christian Reflections*:

I have been reading poems, romances, vision-literature, legends, myths all my life. I know what they are like. I know that not one of them is like this. Of this text there are only two possible views. Either this is reportage – though it may no doubt contain errors – pretty close up to the facts; nearly as close as Boswell. Or else, some unknown writer in the second century, without known predecessors or successors, suddenly anticipated the whole technique of modern, novelistic, realistic narrative. If it is untrue, it must be narrative of that kind. The reader who doesn't see this has simply not learned to read.

I myself studied Homer in depth at Oxford. And I know that the experts in the subject are altogether more willing to allow the material to teach them what happened in the days of the Trojan War than some New Testament scholars are to allow the Gospels to teach them what happened in the life and teaching of Jesus. This is all the more astonishing when you consider the time gap. The Homeric poems were probably first written down in the sixth century BC but they contain material dating back five hundred years before that, and reached written form at the end of a period of oral transmission almost as long. But with the New Testament the oral period is a mere thirty years and the controlling influence of eyewitnesses is still a major factor in the tradition. The analogy with Norse and Homeric myths is one of the most inept to have been foisted upon New Testament studies. Yes, there are indeed frequent methodological errors in the procedures of the sceptics!

Sceptics often display a curious preference for inferior evidence

Many sceptical scholars compare Jesus to the motif of the *theios anēr*, 'divine man', a belief which they assume was commonplace in the ancient world. But there is among these scholars a quite uncritical readiness to imagine that 'divine men' were two a penny in antiquity and furnish a background for the conviction that Jesus was divine. In point of fact, the evidence is both rare and late. The account of the best known of them, Apollonius of Tyana, comes from the end of the second century AD, and is written up by Philostratus, a most unreliable narrator! And yet we are invited to believe that the story of Jesus was fashioned on exemplars such as this.

Take the Gnostic Redeemer Myth. How often we meet him in the writings of sceptical New Testament scholars who are unhappy about the incarnation and the ascension of Jesus. Rarely do they have the honesty to admit that there is no reliable evidence for this supposed Gnostic Redeemer who descends from heaven to rescue the lost, in any pre-Christian material anywhere. And if there was, that would not for one moment invalidate the possibility that God did become a man in order to redeem us. Analogy does not invalidate history.

Take the Acts of the Apostles. In just a couple of places there may be a link between Luke's account and that of Josephus, the Jewish historian who wrote at the end of the first century. It is well known that Josephus was tendentious and at times unreliable. Yet sceptical scholars regularly prefer his version to that of Luke, who has repeatedly been shown, to the satisfaction of Roman historians, to be remarkably accurate in the picture he presents of first-century society. If Luke and Josephus clash, for example over the date of a Jewish freedom fighter called Theudas (Acts 5:36), and it is by no means clear that they do, why should it be Luke who is disbelieved?

Or take the authorship of the Fourth Gospel. As we have seen, there is strong and early evidence that the apostle John wrote this Gospel. Many modern scholars do not think he did. So what do they do? They try to explain away the powerful evidence of Irenaeus and his personal link with John through Polycarp, and prefer the evidence of a ninth-century monk, George the Sinner (who was doubtless not given his nickname for nothing!). If sceptical scholars would show the same scepticism towards the sources they want to follow as those they do not want to follow, the cause of truth would be advanced.

Christian faith is not belief that fairy tales are pleasant, as Bertrand Russell once observed. Faith is self-commitment to Christ on good evidence. The Gospels give us good evidence to warrant that commitment. Indeed, as Søren Kierkegaard pointed out in his *Philosophical Fragments*, we have a great deal more historical evidence about Jesus than we strictly need. If all that had survived from the circle of the disciples was a scrap of papyrus with the testimony that Jesus, through his person, his teaching, his cross and his resurrection had brought God into their midst, and that in trusting their lives to him his disciples had not been let down – that would have sufficed to challenge future generations to make the same experiment of faith. In point of fact, however, we are infinitely richer than that, with the four Gospels which have come down to us from the earliest church, and which tell a story which is utterly awesome but eminently credible.

In a word, undue scepticism about the New Testament record is quite unwarranted.

13. WILL THE REAL JESUS STAND UP?

We have had a good look at many of the calumnies to which Jesus is often subjected and also at more honest objections to Christian claims. He would certainly not be able to stand up if he were just another mythical saviour like Attis or Mithras. He would not be able to stand up if the manuscript attestation to his life and teaching was late or corrupt. He would not be able to stand up if the content of the Gospels revealed a selfish, cruel or arrogant person. Nor could he stand up if the Muslim story was true, that he did not really die on the cross at all. As for the resurrection – well, without it Jesus would long ago have faded away into the history books, instead of boasting a third of humankind as his current followers.

The real Jesus can stand up. He can withstand the criticism that is often heaped upon him. He has been weathering storms of contumely for the past two thousand years, and like a rock pounded by the waves, he stands firm. And why not? For, as the good book puts it, 'Jesus Christ is the same yesterday and today and forever' (Hebrews 13:8).

But there is another sense in which the real Jesus stands up. He stands up for what is beautiful in life, what is true, what is honest, what is pure, what is generous, loving and sacrificial. On any showing his is the most perfect life this world has ever seen. And the further we get away from the ideals he embodied, the less hope there is for the future of our race.

We saw in the Introduction how a distinguished thinker, starting from secularist presuppositions, could maintain that human beings are no different from animals. It would be disastrous for our world if that was the case. Of course, there is much to support the hypothesis. The rape of the environment, the melting of North and South Poles because of our reckless carbon emissions, the pansexuality which characterizes our lifestyle, the greed of rich nations which ensures the continued subjugation of the poor, the slavery in which millions are kept, the propagation of religion by violence, the endless wars – the list could go on. We may not be just the same as animals, but we are not making a very good fist of living in our brave new world.

By way of contrast, the real Jesus stands up as the brightest beacon for society at large. Alas, I cannot make this claim for his followers, who are often narrow-minded, disunited, hypocritical, and have been guilty – indeed still are – of war, oppression, greed and cruelty. I do not for a moment imagine that Christianity can save the world. I make that claim for Jesus alone. His selflessness, his love for other people, his courageous standing up for right, his purity and honesty, must surely be our goal if we are not to tear ourselves apart with our sectional interests, and destroy each other like rats in a cage.

Yes, Jesus can stand up without embarrassment in the critical gaze of other religions and of none. The world has never seen his like, and certainly never his superior. His life and teaching constitute a signpost for mankind, and embody our best, perhaps our only, hope for the future.

But there is yet another way in which the real Jesus can stand up. And it brings a world of encouragement to us as individuals. He is not only the signpost on the way to a better future for the world. He is the engine to move us as individuals in that direction. Authentic Christianity has always maintained that of ourselves we are incapable of following Jesus Christ. We constantly fall short. But the risen Christ offers his unseen power, his Holy Spirit to come within the believer and begin to change him or her into something reminiscent of Jesus himself. The New Testament insists that he wants to make us more like him, and he offers the power of his indwelling Holy Spirit to bring about the necessary changes.

Of course, the job will never be complete in this life, but then Christianity never thought that this life is all there is. There will only be an approximation while we are in this world, but there will be all eternity for development and growth. Here and now there will still be failures of all kinds among Christian people, but as they allow the Spirit of Jesus to have access to every aspect of their lives, there will be transformation – not complete, but substantial. For the real Jesus stands up as the one who loves to take us in our failure and weakness and make new people of us. He is in the transformation business. If you doubt it, why not make an experiment? Ask him to start the transformation in you. Only then will you know its power.

And how could we do that? Perhaps the first thing to get clear is that we can never climb our way up to God. His salvation, or rescue, is entirely due to grace. 'For it is by grace you have been saved, through faith – and this not from yourselves, it is the gift of God – not by works, so that no-one can boast' (Ephesians 2:8–9). Grace is not a word we use much these days – perhaps because there is not a lot of it around. It means 'sheer undeserved generosity'. Here are two stories which may help us to get an understanding of it.

In the grim days of apartheid in South Africa, terrible acts of cruelty and oppression were regularly inflicted on the black population. After black majority rule was established it was crucial to bring reconciliation to a hurting and divided country. So the Justice and Reconciliation Commission was established.

All charges would be dropped if those guilty of atrocities would meet their victims, acknowledge their crimes, and ask for pardon. Many amazing stories came out of that situation. One woman faced the white officer who had tortured her son to death. He acknowledged what he had done with tears of repentance. He cried out for forgiveness. And she not only forgave him, but took him into her home in the place of her son. That is grace!

The other astonishing story is this. It comes from the Bedouin culture of the Middle Eastern deserts. A man rushed, unannounced and dishevelled, into the tent of a Bedouin chieftain. He admitted that he had just killed a man and begged for sanctuary. Hospitality is something very sacred in Arab culture, and the chieftain accepted him and offered him the security he craved. Then in ran a servant who cried, 'The man he killed was your son!' After a long pause the chieftain gave his decision: 'I forgive this man. He shall stay with me and serve in the place of my son.' That is grace!

And it is God's grace that brings us to our knees – which is the right place to start. Jesus said, 'Come to me, all you who are weary and burdened, and I will give you rest. Take my yoke upon you and learn from me . . . For my yoke is easy and my burden is light' (Matthew 11:28–30). I once read of a man asking a clergyman if he could give him a watertight argument for the truth of Christianity. The pastor replied, 'God has not given us a watertight argument, but rather a watertight person.' That's the point. The existence, character, teaching, death and resurrection of Jesus are watertight, despite all the attacks and slurs that have been levelled at him both down the centuries and today. It is this utterly loving and reliable Jesus who invites us into his company. There are three things we need to do by way of response.

The first, as the whole of the New Testament asserts, is repentance. This is a word that is much misunderstood. It is not remorse for things we have done wrong. It is not even the willingness to change, though of course if we have been cheating the company or unfaithful to our marriage partner there must be the willingness for that to change. But there are lots of people who have improved their ethics, but do not have any relationship with Jesus Christ. No, repentance goes deeper than being sorry for past sins. It is a whole new attitude, a complete 'about turn', which is what the Greek word for it means.

Our lives have been self-absorbed, and repentance means willingness for Jesus to come and occupy that central place which we have jealously guarded for ourselves. We have had lots of gods – career, fame, pleasure and the rest. We have prided ourselves on our achievements and our moral virtues. But none of that can get us to God, and repentance admits as much.

The second step is faith, trust in Jesus Christ as the one who can bring us into relationship with the living God. He has made the way clear through his death on the cross to deal with our separation, and through his risen life to equip us for the spiritual battle that becoming a Christian will inevitably involve.

Timothy Keller gives a graphic illustration of this 'saving faith'. In his superb book, *The Reason for God*, he puts it like this:

Imagine you are on a high cliff and you lose your footing and begin to fall. Just beside you as you fall is a branch sticking out of the very edge of the cliff. It is your only hope, and it is more than strong enough to support your weight. How can it save you? If your mind is filled with intellectual certainty that the branch can support you, but you don't actually reach out and grab it, you are lost. If your mind is instead filled with doubts and uncertainty that the branch can hold you, but your reach out and grab it anyway, you will be saved. Why? It is not the strength of your faith but the object of your faith that actually saves you. Strong faith in a weak branch is fatally inferior to weak faith in a strong branch. This means that you don't have to wait for all doubts and fears to go away, to take hold of Christ.

Wise words, and an excellent illustration of authentic faith. Why not here and now transfer your trust from your own achievements to Jesus Christ, and ask him to accept you as his own? He will. And before long the difference will be very plain not only to you but to others.

There is a third requirement that features strongly in the New Testament. It is Christian baptism. This involves public washing in water in the 'name' (or possession) of the Father, the Son and the Holy Spirit. This is not only a very physical demonstration of human faith grasping the sheer grace of God. It is also commitment to a community of believers. You can't be a Christian in secret, and you can't be a Christian on your own. Baptism means beginning with Christ and it also means belonging to his church.

It is a very decisive step. We do not always recognize this in Western lands, where many people are baptized in infancy. But you have only to go to a Hindu or Muslim country to see the decisive nature of the sacrament of baptism. If Hindus or Muslims believe in Jesus privately there is generally not much demur in the community. But they get baptized, then they are often disowned by the family, rejected by the community, and frequently attempts are made on their life. Baptism is rightly seen as the mark of exclusive allegiance to Jesus Christ as Lord.

And it is this commitment to Christ in repentance, faith and baptism that could save our civilization, if only it is adopted both personally and communally. We have examined various calumnies and attacks on the person of Jesus as this book has progressed. They are not important in themselves, but only as they cloud people's eyes to who Jesus, the Saviour of the world, really is. If this book has done anything to blow away the clouds of doubt and misinformation, and allow the real Jesus to stand up, then it is over to the reader to take the next step!

TAKING IT FURTHER: SOME USEFUL RESOURCES

Richard Bauckham, *Jesus and the Eyewitnesses*, Grand Rapids, Michigan: Wm. B. Eerdmans Publishing, 2006.

F. F. Bruce, *The New Testament Documents: Are They Reliable?* Grand Rapids, Michigan: Wm. B. Eerdmans Publishing, 2003.

Craig A. Evans, *Fabricating Jesus: How Modern Scholars Distort the Gospels*, Downers Grove, Illinois: InterVarsity Press, 2006.

Timothy Keller, *The Reason For God*, New York: Dutton, 2008.

Josh McDowell and Bill Wilson, *He Walked Among Us*, San Bernardino, CA: Here's Life Publishers, 1988.

Alister E. McGrath, *Doubt in Perspective: God is Bigger Than You Think*, Leicester: IVP, 2006.

Philip Sampson, *6 Modern Myths About Christianity and Western Civilization*, Downers Grove, Illinois: InterVarsity Press, 2001.

Lee Strobel, *The Case for Christ: A Journalist's Personal Investigation of the Evidence for Jesus*, Grand Rapids, Michigan: Zondervan, 2001.

Lee Strobel, *The Case for Faith: A Journalist Investigates the Toughest Questions to Christianity*, Grand Rapids, Michigan: Zondervan, 2002.

Lee Strobel, *The Case for the Real Jesus: A Journalist Investigates Current Attacks on the Identity of Christ*, Grand Rapids, Michigan: Zondervan, 2007.

Ben Witherington, III, *What Have They Done with Jesus? Beyond Strange Theories and Bad History – Why We Can Trust the Bible*, London: HarperCollins, 2007.

N. T. Wright, *The Resurrection of the Son of God*, London: SPCK Publishing, 2003.

N. T. Wright, *Simply Christian: Why Christianity Makes Sense*, London: HarperCollins, 2006.

Ravi Zacharias, *Jesus Among Other Gods: The Absolute Claims of the Christian Message*, Nashville, TN: Thomas Nelson Inc., 2002.

NOTES

Introduction

7 'The first thing we must learn about him': Lord Hailsham (Quintin Hogg), *The Door Wherein I Went*, London: Collins, 1975.

8 'probably a very hip guy': Interview with John Lennon by Steve Turner, in Steve Turner, *The Gospel according to the Beatles*, Louisville and London: Westminster John Knox Press, 2006, p. 209.

9 'Christians understood history as a story of sin': John Gray, *Straw Dogs – Thoughts on Humans and Other Animals*, London: Granta Books, 2002, p. xiii.

9 'Knowledge does not make us free': John Gray, ibid., p. xiv.

9 'Darwin showed that humans are like': John Gray, ibid., p. 4.

9 'But if Darwin's theory of natural selection': John Gray, ibid., p. 26.

9 'Christianity's cardinal error – the belief ': John Gray, ibid., p. 37.

10 'the upshot of neuroscientific research is': John Gray, ibid., p. 67.

Chapter 1. The Jesus We Thought We Knew

26 'Without the resurrection there would have been': Pinchas Lapide, *The Resurrection of Jesus*, London: SPCK, 1984 pp. 126, 149.

Chapter 2. 'Scholars are Discovering a Very Different Jesus'

36 *'Thomas's* Jesus directs each disciple to discover': Elaine Pagels, *Beyond Belief: the Secret Gospel of Thomas*, New York: Random House Inc., 2004, p. 68.

45 'trying to smuggle into the first century a mystical': Craig
   Evans, quoted in *The Case for the Real Jesus*, Lee Strobel,
   Grand Rapids, Michigan: Zondervan, p. 35.

Chapter 3. 'Jesus Had a Fling With Mary Magdalene'

52 'And the companion of the Saviour is Mary': Dan
   Brown, *The Da Vinci Code*, London: Corgi Books, 2004,
   p. 331.
55 'the apostles were considered to be guarantors': Karen
   King, *Gospel of Mary Magdalene: Jesus and the First Woman
   Apostle*, Santa Rosa, CA: Polebridge Press, 2003, p. 167.

Chapter 4. 'Jesus? He's Just a Myth'

58 'there is nothing the Jesus of the Gospels either said or did':
   Tom Harpur, *The Pagan Christ: Is Blind Faith Killing
   Christianity?* Sydney: Allen and Unwin, 2005, p. 10.
58 'Why should we consider the stories of Osiris': Timothy
   Freke and Peter Gandy, *The Jesus Mysteries: Was the "Original
   Jesus" a Pagan God?* New York: Three Rivers Press, 2001,
   p. 9.
69 'No search for parallels has given us': Raymond E. Brown,
   The Virginal Conception and Bodily Resurrection of Jesus, New
   York: Paulist Press, 1973, p. 65.

Chapter 5. 'The New Testament manuscripts are unreliable'

79 'The interval, then, between the dates of original
   composition': Sir Frederic Kenyon, *The Bible and Archaeology*,
   London: George Harrap, 1940, pp. 288–9.

Chapter 6. 'The New Testament story is incredible'

87 'Matthew compiled the Logia in the Hebrew': Eusebius,
   H.E. 3.39.

92 'The Synoptists may give us something more like the perfect photograph': William Temple, *Readings in St John's Gospel*, London: Macmillan, 1947, p. xvi.

93 'If God creates a miraculous spermatozoon in the body': C. S. Lewis, *Miracles: A Preliminary Study*, London: Fontana, 1960, Revised edition, pp. 63–64.

Chapter 7. 'Jesus never really went to the cross!'

98 'They said (in boast) "We killed Christ Jesus the Son of Mary"': The Qu'ran, sura 4.156f., translation of Abdullah Yusuf Ali.

Chapter 8. 'Jesus did not rise from the dead – his tomb has been found!'

103 'The proposal that Jesus': N. T. Wright, *The Resurrection of the Son of God*, London: SPCK, 2003.

105 'Their movie is not serious': 'Jesus' Tomb Claim Slammed By Scholars', *National Geographic News*, February 28, 2007, *http://news.nationalgeographic.com/news/2007/02/070228-jesus-tomb.html.*

Chapter 9. 'Jesus did not rise from the dead – there's no evidence'

111 'This is the Christ-bit, you know': interview with Steve Turner 1971, Steve Turner, *The Gospel According to the Beatles*, Kentucky: Westminster John Knox Press, 2006, pp. 209–10.

119 'Whatever may be thought of the Gospel records': J. M. Roberts, *History of Europe*, London: Penguin, 1996, p. 63.

125 'Can the resurrection narratives': Rudolf Bultmann, *Kerygma and Myth: A Theological Debate*, London: SPCK, 1953, pp. 38, 42.

129 'forced open a door that had been locked': C. S. Lewis, *Miracles: A Preliminary Study*, London: Geoffrey Bles, the Centenary Press, 1947.

Chapter 10. 'Nobody thought Jesus divine until the fourth century'

131 'natural and intelligible that Jesus': John Hick (Ed.), *The Myth of God Incarnate*, Philadelphia: Westminster Press, 1977, p. ix.

132 'that many aspects of Christianity were debated and voted upon': Dan Brown, *The Da Vinci Code*, London: Corgi Books, 2004, p. 315.

132 'To rewrite the history books, Constantine knew': Dan Brown, ibid., pp. 316–317.

Chapter 11. 'The "New" Testament is evil'

147 'a work of crude carpentry, hammered together': Christopher Hitchens, *God is Not Great: How Religion Poisons Everything*, Sydney: Allen & Unwin, 2007, p. 110.

147 'The simple fact is that the New Testament': H. L. Mencken, quoted in Christopher Hitchens, ibid., p. 110.

150 'Their multiple authors – none of whom published anything': Christopher Hitchens, ibid., p. 111.

157 'Once again we have a father demonstrating love': Christopher Hitchens, ibid., p. 249.

158 'I am required to believe that the agony': Christopher Hitchens, ibid., p. 250.

161 'These scrolls were of the same period and provenance': Christopher Hitchens, ibid., p. 112.

162 'Many Christians believe that Jesus did away with all this barbarism': Sam Harris, *Letter to a Christian Nation*, New York: Bantam, 2007, p. 10.

164 'Jesus said some profound things about love': Sam Harris, ibid., p. 10.

Chapter 12. The real trouble with scepticism about the Jesus story

171 'I have been reading poems, romances, vision-literature': C. S. Lewis, *Christian Reflections*, London: Geoffrey Bles, 1967, p. 155.

Chapter 13. Will the real Jesus stand up?

179 'Imagine you are on a high cliff and you lose your footing': Timothy Keller, *The Reason For God*, New York: Dutton, 2008, p. 234

Also by Michael Green

MICHAEL GREEN & NICK SPENCER

'Religious people are too intolerant.'
'You can't trust what is in the Bible.'
'Science has disproved Christianity.'
'There's too much suffering in the world.'
'Something 2,000 years ago can't be relevant to me today.'

Michael Green has responded to each of these statements in a direct and informal way, giving his Christian perspective on the opinions expressed. His easy style engages readers and shows how the Bible and Christian beliefs can provide a real faith for life. This book may even help you believe in spite of your buts ...

'Based on real questions from real people in the real world. I would recommend this book to anyone investigating what Christianity is all about, and, as ever from Michael Green, it's brilliant stuff!'
— **Andy Hawthorne,**
Director of The Message Trust

'Michael Green pulls no punches as he answers the voices of modern unbelief with love, humour and the power of Scripture-based scholarship. Authentic on both sides, the contrast makes compelling reading.'
— **Jonathan Aitken,**
author, broadcaster and former Cabinet Minister

ISBN:
978-1-84474-390-2

Available from your local Christian bookshop or via our website at **www.ivpbooks.com**

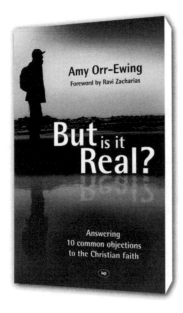

www.ivpbooks.com

For more details of books published by IVP, visit our website where you will find all the latest information, including:

Book extracts   Downloads
Author interviews   Online bookshop
Reviews   Christian bookshop finder

You can also sign up for our regular email newsletters, which are tailored to your particular interests, and tell others what you think about this book by posting a review.

We publish a wide range of books on various subjects including:

Christian living   Small-group resources
Key reference works   Topical issues
Bible commentary series Theological studies